WILLIAM THE SECOND

AS SEEN IN CONTEMPORARY
DOCUMENTS AND JUDGED ON
EVIDENCE OF HIS OWN SPEECHES

BY

S. C. HAMMER, M.A.

BOSTON AND NEW YORK
HOUGHTON MIFFLIN COMPANY
1917

CONTENTS

CHAPTER		PAGE
I.	YOUTH	1
II.	FATHER AND SON	14
III.	THE YOUNG RULER	28
IV.	JOURNEYS AND INTRIGUES	42
V.	THE BREACH WITH BISMARCK	53
VI.	THE NEW MASTER	67
VII.	AN ENLIGHTENED POLICY	81
VIII.	POLITICAL CHESS	95
IX.	THE JUBILEE YEAR	106
X.	A FUTURE ON THE SEAS	120
XI.	THE END OF THE FIRST TEN YEARS	131
XII.	THEORY AND FACT	145
XIII.	THE TRIUMPH OF CÆSARISM	157
XIV.	DISAPPOINTMENTS	173
XV.	THE *METEOR* AND OTHERS	187
XVI.	NERVOUS SYMPTOMS	201
XVII.	AN INTERVIEW AND ITS CONSEQUENCES	215
XVIII.	BEFORE THE GREAT WAR	228
XIX.	WILLIAM THE PROBLEM	243
	LITERATURE CONCERNING WILLIAM II.	263
	INDEX	265

CHAPTER I

YOUTH

DURING the last days of 1858 great political unrest, associated in a singular manner with simple-hearted loyalty, was prevalent in Berlin and throughout Prussia.

The rule of the childless Frederick William IV had presented for many years an almost unique picture of incapacity and wilfulness; during 1857 he had been obliged, on account of failing mental powers, to relinquish all State business, and was at the moment living in Italy, a chronic invalid. His brother, Prince William, who acted as Regent, was still a political novice, in spite of his sixty odd years, and it was Bismarck who was destined to place him amongst the historic figures of the age. For the time being, however, he was preeminently the Prince of the *petite bourgeoisie*, the unpretentious ideal of the ordinary public who frequented tea-gardens and beerhouses; while those in leading positions were obliged to recognize that he had neither much political capacity nor even a strong personality.

With the dawn of the New Year fresh troubles arose. At the New Year's levée in the Tuileries, Napoleon III expressed his regret to the Austrian

Ambassador that friendly relations no longer existed between the French and Austrian Governments, and this ominous observation—made in the hearing of the whole Diplomatic Corps—blazed like a beacon of war from one country to another. Nowhere, with the exception of Vienna, was the news received with more excitement than at Berlin, as indeed was only natural. The Prussian Government was subjected to violent pressure from Austria, both by means of diplomacy and through the Press ; but in spite of every provocation, Berlin maintained an obstinate silence for several months, evidently because the time was not considered opportune for that national war that should end in German unity. A policy of this kind is apt to result in a condition of a public apprehension, and it was therefore a kindly dispensation of Providence that a pleasing diversion from so much anxiety shortly presented itself.

The Prince Regent's only son, Prince Frederick William of Prussia, had married in 1857 the Princess Royal of Great Britain, eldest daughter of Queen Victoria. At first the alliance was not very popular, either in England or in Prussia ; but now, when it had been announced that the Princess was expecting a child, all classes of society united heartily in their good wishes towards her.

The event, which was expected to take place during the latter half of January, aroused extraordinary excitement. It became the central point in Church prayers, and was the main topic of conversation both in family circles and at public gatherings. As an official chronicler tells us : " All social engagements were postponed in expectation of the day that should secure a successor to the throne, and the coming event was eagerly awaited by every one." A whole nation, as it were, walked on tiptoe outside the nursery door.

On Tuesday, January 25, 1859, the event was so close at hand that two batteries of artillery were ready in their barracks, prepared to fire the salute the moment the news should be received.

It came at a little after three on the afternoon of the 27th January. But even before the salute was fired the news had spread like wildfire through the capital, "Es ist ein Prinz." Those who were still in ignorance counted the guns up to thirty-six, and thus all doubts were dispelled.

"Es ist ein Prinz!" These words passed throughout the city like a word of command. In a few hours Berlin was transformed. Every house was decorated with flags and streamers—many Union Jacks among them—and at night there was a general illumination that extended to the remotest quarters of the city. Unter den Linden was one great sea of human beings, and in all the places of amusement rejoicings knew no bounds. In the provinces enthusiasm was equally great, and even in London the public caught the fever.[1] The next day newspapers in

[1] The following contemporary verse is not without a certain interest at the present time :—

> Hail the auspicious morn!
> To Prussia's throne is born
> A royal heir.
>
> May he defend its laws
> Join with old England's cause,
> Thus win all men's applause!

every country devoted leading articles to the event, and there was a sudden amazing increase in the number of German poets.

Five weeks later the little Prince was christened, receiving the names of Friedrich Wilhelm Victor Albert—in token of his German and British descent. According to all contemporary records, the succeeding weeks were very busy ones for Berlin. Prince William's birth was the central point round which existence revolved. "The politicians who discuss the event exhibit their enthusiasm more than their tact or decency," wrote a contemporary British correspondent. "All the ladies of Berlin talk about nurses, and the newspapers are full of articles on midwifery. Princess Victoria is the darling of the hour. Everything she does or says is repeated, applauded, and imitated. The colour of her ribbons, the shape of her collars, are copied with the most touching fidelity." After giving other instances of this extravagant enthusiasm—which, we are told, affected one minor poet so strongly that he exhorted the infant of a few weeks "to place the crown of Germany without delay upon his head"—the writer concluded by quoting a lullaby with the somewhat monotonous refrain "Su! Su! Su!" "It is immensely popular," he added; "but we will not attempt to translate it, as it would lose too much of its beauty."

After the christening on March 5th things began to settle down again. The congratulations and deputations ceased; the illuminations died down and the torches were extinguished. The happy parents conveyed their thanks to the nation in a letter to the *Gazette*, and concluded by expressing the hope that "we shall be enabled by God's help to bring up our son to be an honour and blessing to our beloved country."

Before many years had gone by they found that this task was fraught with difficulties.

From an early age Prince William showed great wilfulness, a characteristic which stood out in marked contrast to his slight, almost girlish appearance, and to a certain physical awkwardness, due to an unfortunate want of power in the left arm. As the years went by his wilfulness increased, and asserted itself much during his lessons. Everything connected with outward forms and social success—for instance, foreign languages—he acquired with almost incredible facility. With an energy that was no less striking, and with an inborn indifference to bodily discomfort, he struggled at an early age to overcome that handicap in physical exercises occasioned by his useless arm. On the other hand, it was very hard to make him respond to any moral or spiritual influence, and, on the whole, he was what people call " a difficult child." His inability to fix his thoughts on any special subject was very marked, and " neither his gifted mother, his wise, tolerant father, nor his philosophical tutor were able to exercise the least influence on the boy in this respect," says his tutor, Dr. Hintzpeter. Those in charge of the Prince made especial efforts to counteract the evil effects of the " flood of thought and impressions that stream into the minds of all princes from their earliest childhood, and which are so apt to result in confusion of thought and satiety of feeling." It was therefore essential that " all those in authority should exercise the greatest firmness and should work loyally and energetically together"; but even this "strong pressure of moral force methodically applied" appears to have had no permanent influence on the future Kaiser. "Now and then," adds Dr. Hintzpeter, "it appeared as if we had succeeded, and many hopes were raised. But in a short time they were dispelled, and our disappointment was all the greater when we discovered that his original character remained unaltered."

No great discernment is necessary to realize that a prince and heir-apparent with a character of the kind described could not fail to be in a difficult position in the Germany of the 'sixties. The nation was then passing through its heroic age. Little by little it had secured all that for generations it had yearned for, and all classes of society had contributed to this work. The prominent figures of the time were essentially men of action who commanded public attention by their practical gifts, and also by a certain touch of imagination which never ran away with them, and yet which threw a glamour over their actions and gave them power to penetrate the national consciousness. Prince William saw nothing of all this, nor indeed had he any natural tendency to be attracted by it. As far as he was concerned, the whole thing was a military spectacle, a triumphal march with glittering arms and martial music. His grandfather and all the " paladins," with the exception of Bismarck, were his childish heroes, and his boyish imagination had invented his own legend as to how it all came about. His parents saw with dismay how these military propensities threatened to gain a complete mastery over him, and they did all in their power to counteract them by putting forward the interests of civil life. They adopted various means—as, for instance, frequent tours both in their own country and abroad—and utilized every available opportunity to this end. Later on—towards the end of his boyhood—they went so far against all tradition as to send their son to a " gymnasium " at Kassel, where he spent his time from September 1874 to January 1877 amidst entirely civil surroundings. He visited factories and museums, workshops and mines ; he learned to know the life of the people at their various occupations, and caught a glimpse of the importance of each man's work for the good of all. At the same time, he began to show those scientific and technical interests—tastes inherited from his British mother—which in the course of time were to develop in so striking a manner, in many instances enabling him to astonish even real authorities on the subject.

In a letter from Prince William, written in 1885, we find a number of statements that throw light both upon himself and upon the system of public-school education in vogue in Germany at that time, although it should be borne in mind that his picture was very quickly pronounced somewhat one-sided by German scholastic authorities. He brands the gymnasium system as "the most antiquated and soul-destroying of all systems," and mentions as a characteristic example that " out of twenty-one boys in my class nineteen wore spectacles, and of the nineteen three were actually obliged to hold an eyeglass in front of their spectacles when they wished to read what was on the blackboard!"

The methods of teaching appear to have been on a par with the rest of the system.

"Homer, that splendid genius, whom I admire so much; Horace, Demosthenes, whose speeches cannot fail to arouse enthusiasm—how were they read? Perhaps, you say, with keen delight in the glorious conflicts, or it may be in the descriptions of Nature? Alas no! Beneath the scalpel of a pedantic and fanatical philologist every little sentence was divided and subdivided, until the skeleton was found and exhibited with much pride for general admiration. . . . It is enough to make one weep. And the Latin and Greek exercises—what folly they were! What labour and toil they cost us! And yet what rubbish the results were! Away with such lumber! Let us wage war to the knife against such teaching! The result of the system is that our children know Greek syntax better than the Greeks themselves: that they know by heart the lists of generals, battles, and positions in the Punic and Mithridatic wars, but have only a vague idea of the battles of the Seven Years War or even the modern wars of 1866 and 1870, which they have not yet had for their examinations!" As regards physical exercise, he advises drill under the charge of a non-commissioned officer in all towns where soldiers are quartered, and "instead of the so-called class promenades with walking-sticks, black coats, and cigars, route marches, with a little field exercise, even though it may degenerate into horseplay and fisticuffs."

In spite of this scathing criticism of teachers and their methods, there is good reason for believing that his remarks must partly be ascribed to an outburst of feeling dictated by the desire to put in a word on a much-discussed question, and to do so in the sensational and confident manner that has always been one of the Kaiser's characteristics. If this were not so, it would be even more difficult than it is to reconcile these statements with those made at Kassel many years later, in which he observed that it was precisely the " serious and incessant studies that I pursued at the gymnasium here . . . which have enabled me to bear those burdens that grow heavier from day to day."

He expressed a similar feeling of gratitude when he took leave of the school. We are told that at a farewell dinner he proposed the health of the teachers and school in well-chosen words. The members of the staff all received a decoration, and all the boys in the Prince's form received a cabinet photograph of their royal class-mate, " in civil dress or uniform as preferred," and inscribed with his autograph on the back.

One of his teachers presented him with an ode, in which he was compared to young Alexander, who, far from the noise of the world outside, prepared himself for his future vocation, " to conquer the world with sudden swiftness and lay the foundation of lasting fame amongst future generations by the memory of his great prowess."

From the gymnasium at Kassel his path led

him to the University of Bonn, where for two years he studied an absolutely bewildering number of subjects. He attended lectures on Roman law, history, philosophy, experimental physics, the history of the nineteenth century, the history of German government and German law, political economy, ancient art, modern German literature, criminal law and procedure, finance, the history of art, the history of the Reformation, national and international law, chemistry, and, lastly, politics and the Prussian administrative system! This list conveys some idea of his appetite for knowledge and his difficulty in concentrating his mind. As a German author remarks: " It stands to reason that it was not possible for the Prince to be attracted and captivated in an equal degree by all those various subjects and by the many different methods of instruction prevailing at the University." Expressed less pompously, this means that several of the subjects mentioned above—for example, German literature and ancient and modern art—were taken very superficially, not more than one term being devoted to each. Under these circumstances it is easy to explain why the Kaiser's admiration for Goethe, whom he otherwise recognizes as a great man of genius, has always been quite impersonal, and why he should regard Schiller as a revolutionary whose influence as an author was not entirely evil, or again, how he can discern the greatness of a Renaissance in the modern Berlin school of sculpture.

As far as he personally is concerned, he has often said that he considers his time at Bonn to have been one of the happiest in his life, and as a member of the famous "Borusser" Corps he made many friends, a circumstance that is significant because of the affection he has always retained for his companions of that time. It is thus no mere chance, for instance, that the present Chancellor Bethmann-Hollweg, the Foreign Minister von Jagow, and that unofficial counsellor the multi-millionaire Prince Fürstenberg, were one and all college friends of the Kaiser.

"In the midst of this active intercourse in school, University, and the life of the people," writes Dr. Hintzpeter, "his interest in military matters developed so rapidly that at length it occupied the first place in his dreams, his thoughts, and his actions." Many minor incidents of his boyhood and youth confirm this statement, and the atmosphere of military tradition in which he lived necessarily contributed in no small degree to the development of that side of his nature which his wise parents strove in vain to check.

"It is a prerogative of princes of the House of Hohenzollern," said the Kaiser in a speech made in 1899, "that from the age of ten they learn to offer their strength and their energy to the service of the Fatherland."

In accordance with this family tradition, the little Prince William in 1869 received a commission as lieutenant in the Footguards, after four years' training as a sergeant. In the same year he paraded for the first time before his grandfather, wearing his new uniform and decorated with the Black Eagle. King William, who had not yet reached the summit of his military fame, spoke a few words to his grandson after the parade, and expressed the hope that the boy "might live to look back on a long period of service and share further glories in the history of this gallant regiment." As was the case with all his grandfather's utterances, these words were indelibly printed in the boy's memory, and more than once in the history of William II the 1st Footguards have played an important part, not merely in military affairs but also in those of a political character.

The following year saw the great event that led to the unification of the Empire—the Franco-German War, with all its dramatic incidents. One message of victory after another was proclaimed in Germany: Weissenburg, Wörth, Gravelotte, Sedan, only to name the greatest. An Empire associated with the most glorious name in modern European history lay in ruins, and a new Empire was to arise, with the Hohenzollerns at its head. Napoleon's comet had burned out like the Revolution which had bred it. But the star of the Hohenzollerns shone bright as Arcturus in the northern sky, royal and calm by virtue of its Divine origin. Subsequent history has revealed certain events connected with the reconstruction of Germany that make the whole impression less sublime than it appeared to contemporary writers. But for the boy growing up in those days it was romance become reality.

Little Prince William was allowed to take part in the final scene. In the triumphal procession through Berlin, June 16, 1871, he rode on a piebald pony along Unter den Linden just behind his father, beside his uncle, the Grand Duke of

Baden. This event made a lasting impression on him, and though there is little reason to believe—as certain Court chroniclers assert—that even at that early period of his life he had already begun to ponder the responsibilities of the Imperial crown, there is much evidence to prove that the splendour of it all held him spellbound.

It is against this historic and psychological background that his schooldays at Kassel and his undergraduate years at Bonn must be contemplated. They were only steps in his education, necessary stages of knowledge through which he had to pass before he could devote himself wholly to that task which, in his eyes, was the greatest of all, and, in fact, the only one that life could offer.

As for education, in 1879, at the age of twenty, he had done with the whole thing. The insignificant school and college days were a thing of the past, and in their place came the Army, with all its seductive splendour of command.

CHAPTER II

FATHER AND SON

SOME years before the completion of his University career—at a time when he was not yet able to devote himself entirely to the Army—Prince William received the following advice from his grandfather on the occasion of his entry upon military service: " In the career upon which you are now about to enter you will observe many things that are apparently insignificant, and this will probably seem strange to you ; but you will learn that in the Service there is nothing trifling, and that every stone required in building an army must be properly shaped if the whole structure is to stand firm and strong."

These words, which were taken almost too literally, became the Prince's motto from the day of his first independent command in 1879, and continued to be so until he finally appeared in the character of "Supreme War-Lord." On marches and parades, at manœuvres and daily drills, he displayed an interest and enthusiasm that aroused public attention and gratified no one more than his aged grandfather. Now and then he had an opportunity of speaking in public, e.g. during some march when his detachment passed a spot of historic interest, or when it fell to his lot to be present at some memorial ceremony of a military character. The facts he related on such occasions were not always as strictly historical as could be wished, but his intentions were excellent ; and who would be too critical towards a young patriotic officer because in the excitement of the moment he makes the vanquished opponents of his country somewhat more formidable than they actually were?

Moreover, the young Prince had independent ideas. At a very early age—he tells us in a speech delivered at the beginning of the 'nineties—he chose as his model the famous Frederick William of Brandenburg, who is known to history as the " Great Elector." The Prince reverenced this man, who was born at the beginning of the Thirty Years War, and who when little more than twenty years of age had succeeded to a patrimony that had been ravaged and scourged by the barbarism of the times. Trampled fields, burnt villages, a starved and perishing population, such was the Brandenburg that Frederick William inherited. But by an iron will and a steadfast piety, he succeeded in welding his country together and in creating that Army which was to prove itself the finest weapon in the struggle for national unity. The Elector had even some maritime ambitions— a wonderful thing in those days, and one of which his subjects could not understand the importance. So it happened that the Navy he created soon dwindled away. " But," said the Kaiser, " the young, whose inheritance is in the future, should fix their eyes upon the Great Elector, and, like him, be God-fearing and severe, exorably severe, towards themselves and towards others ; and, like him also, look upon every disappointment as a trial sent by Heaven."

This picture is noticeably idealized and gives us little or no idea of the autocrat Frederick William, who placed himself above all constitutional considerations and created that arbitrary attitude towards popular representation which afterwards became a Prussian tradition. But it shows us the direction of the young Prince's thoughts, the ideals he cherished, and the questions that were active in his brain.

It is a rule of more than two centuries' standing in Prussia that the Heir-Apparent is to have less power and influence than any private citizen. He may, of course, have interests and sympathies like anybody else and he may study military matters or politics. But he is obliged to be strictly neutral, and must on no account take any part whatever in public discussion or express opinions on the actual questions of the day.

To a nature like that of Prince William such a position would naturally present some difficulties, and it is therefore not surprising to find that before long he began to run counter to tradition.

"Prince William is a somewhat boyish and petulant young man," writes Prince Hohenlohe, afterwards Chancellor of the Empire, in his diary for 1881, some months after the Prince's marriage with Princess Augusta Victoria of Schleswig-Holstein, the present Kaiserin. "His mother is afraid of him, and he also comes into conflict with his father, but his wife is said to exercise a restraining influence."

This description is interesting, though hardly correct with regard to the mother. The future Empress Frederick, with her temperament, was hardly likely to stand in any fear of her son. She saw herself again in his manifold interests and in his keen appreciation of contemporary thought, but she sought in vain for the critical gifts that were so notably her own strength. Prince William could impress others, but under those searching maternal eyes he was powerless.

His father was in the same position, liberal and unprejudiced, filled by the same sense of duty that he observed in his son, but, like his wife, not to be deceived by any exaggerated ideas.

Prince William's knowledge of war was limited to the history of his forefathers, for what little he himself had experienced was confined to victorious dispatches and triumphal processions, passing through streets gay with flowers and flags. He remembered music and colours, sparkling eyes, everything that could appeal to imagination and summon to fresh deeds and fresh glories. His father had experienced the realities of war in three campaigns, and its horrors had left an ineffaceable impression on his memory. "War," he said once in the course of a conversation—"you speak so lightly of war. That is because you have never seen it. Ah! if you had only seen war!"

It was a defect in the Imperial circle that there was no intimate connection between the Court and the actual determining influences of the day. William I was and remained a soldier's emperor just as he had formerly been a soldier's king, and it is well known that throughout his long life his interest in artists and scholars was extremely limited. Kaiserin Augusta had direct traditions from Goethe's Weimar, but unfortunately they were already more than sixty years behind the times, and, as a matter of fact, had never made much difference to her views of life. At the Court of the Crown Prince there was a fresher atmosphere. Interests here were many and varied, even though they did not go very far in a scholarly direction ; and it will always stand to the credit of the Crown Princess of those days that she opened her drawing-room to men like Helmholtz, Virchow, and other representatives of intellectual liberty, thereby doing her best to break the domination of the military idea. This was much to be desired, especially after her son had married and set up a Court of his own, for there the old Kaiser's Court was revived in a new garb. The prevailing note was stiff militarism coupled with strict orthodoxy, the two most influential representatives of these ideas being the anti-Semitic Stoecker and Count Waldersee, afterwards field-marshal.

These divergencies within the royal house inevitably led to collisions and provided material for gossip, whilst at the same time it became evident to every one with the ability and will to form an independent judgment that Prince William's enthusiasm for his grandfather was carrying him far from the province of reality.

The result was that the public occupied itself with him more and more. In some quarters great things were prophesied of him, although it is difficult, not to say impossible, to refer to any authoritative statement to this effect. People drew attention to his mental and physical energy, his love of travel—which even at that time was very marked—his martial and strictly Prussian views of history, all of which seemed to promise a future full of military glory. His love of the sea, an inheritance from his British mother, gave that future a wider horizon. In contrast to his fellow-officers at Potsdam, amongst whom, nevertheless, he was extremely happy, he had none of the prejudice that most of them entertained against the Navy, and by means of academic lectures on the Fleet and its importance, he endeavoured to induce the military officers to regard it with impartial eyes, and to see in it, not a rival but an ally in the great work of national defence.

All this was excellent. But there were those who remarked also certain serious blemishes in his character, such as his unbounded self-esteem, which often took the form of a want of due consideration for others, and his ubiquitous restlessness, which never failed to have some new item on the programme and never forgot to inform the public of it.

Even in relation to a man like Bismarck, whose genius the Prince appreciated at that period of his life, although evidently he never rightly understood the real man, he at times allowed himself to behave with a most extraordinary mixture of familiarity and disrespect, for which it is not easy to find the right word.

On Prince Bismarck's sixty-ninth birthday, in 1884, he was presented by the Prince with the royal photograph, endorsed with the significant

Latin inscription, *Cave! Adsum!* [1] Bismarck laughed superciliously. "Apparently our young friend does not know how rude he is. Youth—yes, youth, believes itself more formidable than it really is. But I agree with Mephistopheles—it may turn into something in the long run."

The quotation is admirable, not least so because it is placed in the mouth of the very representative of doubt and scorn, and it remains a question whether after all Bismarck was not the ruder of the two.

There is an account given by the late Professor Maurenbrecher, of Bonn—Prince William's most distinguished teacher during his years of study—which materially assists us in understanding the Prince's attitude. The professor was simply horrified at his pupil's views of history and politics, and exerted himself to the utmost to instil into his royal charge a different conception of these subjects. But it is evident that he did not succeed. Prince William retained as a man the same primitive ideas of history that he had adopted when a boy. Every event was to be traced to the inspired rulers, the men of action, who at their supreme discretion chose the helpers they might need. The conception of a national soul that has evolved according to its own laws has always been foreign to his mind, and the numerous questions that are closely connected with the economic and social enterprises of the day have never been able to win more than superficial attention from the Kaiser.

The result was that during this important period

[1] Beware! I am here!

of his life, when out of regard to his future vocation it was of the utmost consequence for him to acquire impartial views of the realities of history and of life, Prince William at once wrapped himself in a world of princely romance that belonged to the twelfth century rather than the nineteenth. The Imperial position was Divine and responsible to God alone, and the most burning questions of the day—political, social, economic, even scientific or literary—should first be brought before the intellectual judgment-seat of the Emperor. There alone their triumph or failure would be finally decided. There was something almost disquieting in such an unbounded love of power. Words and metaphors poured from his lips, and, as Dr. Hintzpeter said, his character matured " with almost tropical rapidity."

With this primitive conception of the position of Prince and people, it goes without saying that it never for one instant occurred to the Prince to study politics in the real meaning of the term. Bismarck could have told him that there is no more difficult science, dealing as it does with living, changing values. He could have taught him that the secret of political success rests on a basis of common sense, joined to a certain imaginative power of grasping new situations, and an unflinching determination to reach the great goal. But all this meant nothing to a young man who had no sense of historical perspective, and who, even at the age of twenty-nine, had no practical knowledge of the machinery of State.

It is significant to observe that it was Bismarck who took the first steps in the matter.

In December 1887 the Crown Prince of Prussia was pronounced by the doctors to be incurable, and this was the prelude to an epoch of mental and physical suffering that will always remain one of the saddest memories of the house of Hohenzollern. The old Kaiser was at that time over ninety, and in view of the situation created by the illness of the Crown Prince, Bismarck considered it imperative that Prince William should by degrees be introduced to the details of practical administration.

The old Kaiser was quite in favour of such an arrangement, as he shows by one of his letters to Bismarck, but it was very difficult to adjust the matter. The Crown Prince had already been painfully affected by the circumstance that when the Emperor was prevented from so doing, Prince William took on himself to sign current reports from the civil and military Cabinet under the inscription *By Supreme Command*. If he also began to deal with real matters of State, the Crown Prince would undoubtedly find it even more difficult to reconcile himself to the position. It would look as if they were trying to replace him. Therefore the Kaiser considered it would be best to keep to the old plan, except that during the course of the winter Prince William should have opportunities of becoming acquainted with the work of the Treasury, the Foreign Office, and perhaps also the Home Office, the work in the first instance to be voluntary. "I beg you to give me your opinion on this matter," he concluded in a letter that bears traces of increasing feebleness both of heart and brain.

Bismarck gave no answer, very naturally because he could not well make any objection to the proposal, and the aged Kaiser did not return to the matter.

Four months later William I was no more. On the throne, stricken by a mortal illness, was his son, who had returned from San Remo as Kaiser Frederick III.

It was a strange situation, and one to arouse compassion even in a nation whose feudal traditions were less marked than those of Germany. Crown Prince William correctly expressed these feelings during an after-dinner speech, when he was Bismarck's guest on the occasion of the latter's seventy-third birthday:—

"To use a military illustration, we are in the position of a regiment advancing to the attack. The commander has fallen and the second in command lies dangerously wounded. In this critical moment forty-six million faithful German hearts turn anxiously and hopefully to the flag and its bearer and depend entirely on him. The standard-bearer is our distinguished Prince, our great Chancellor. May he lead us. We will follow him. Long may he live!"

The ninety-nine days that composed the reign of Frederick III were marked by so many tragic details, both bodily and spiritual, such great and heroic suffering, and such slight comforts and consolations, that it is hardly possible to find any parallel to them.

The new Kaiser reached Berlin on March 11th —two days after his father's death—so sorely stricken by his terrible throat affection that, for the time being, he was not able, or at least was not allowed, to speak. One of the first things that had to be announced to the nation was that the ceremony of taking the oath was postponed indefinitely. But outwardly he was hardly changed —his attitude erect, his step remarkably elastic; only his face was paler.

His proclamation to "my people" (i.e. the Prussians) was characterized by the strength of will and spirit that supported him throughout his illness, and in his rescript to Bismarck of the same date there is an unqualified recognition of the Chancellor's great services in the cause of national unity, and, above all, of his guiding influence upon the late Emperor. One is involuntarily tempted to institute a comparison between this view and that which was subsequently expressed by the present Kaiser. The Emperor Frederick regarded Bismarck as his father's "brave and faithful counsellor, who inspired his political aims and secured for them a happy realization." William II again and again during his twenty-five years of rule has tried to establish an idea that is quite without historic foundation—namely, that his grandfather was the original spirit with the wide outlook, and that he took Bismarck into his service at the right psychological moment so that the Chancellor might embody those great thoughts that had so long been prepared in his royal mind.

The remainder of the rescript refers in an impartial manner to various social questions, with an emphasis upon education in particular—as being the most important of all for the younger generation. It is also interesting to note that it is the Kaiser's hope that he "may be able to assist the development of German arts and sciences to that high level of which they now give such ample promise." But above all, he says, without concerning himself about the glamour of great deeds and the fame that comes from them, he will be content if some day it may be said of his government that "it was beneficial to my people, useful to my country, and a blessing to my kingdom."

As we know, it was not long before this admirable conception, with its many fair hopes, was laid aside for ever; but the support that was granted to it, the opposition it encountered, and the bitterness which characterized public life in Germany during the period between William I and William II are the best proofs of the conflicting ideas that prevailed at that time. There were, in fact, two ways of looking at life—represented by the Emperor Frederick and the Crown Prince William—which clashed with one another, and it is remarkable that it was the older man's idea that was most friendly to progress and development. In their youth the Emperor Frederick and his contemporaries had seen the powerlessness of an absolute monarch by Divine right, and they had learned to value the significance of the power of the people and the unlimited creative forces which exist in a nation. On the other hand, the Crown Prince and the men of his age had their impressions formed at a time when the will of the people had been checked and one single overwhelming personality in his own self-chosen way—"not with speeches and the voice of the majority, but with blood and iron "—

had led the nation forward into that unity for which it had yearned during so many years and which it had despaired of ever seeing.

As far as Bismarck was concerned, he was then, as always, quite determined to have a free hand at home and abroad, or, as he himself said, "No parliamentary government and no outside interference in politics." Such were his conditions even three years before, when for a time it seemed as if the old Kaiser would succumb to an illness from which he was then suffering. In the eyes of both parties, therefore, Bismarck was the man who first and foremost must be defeated. Those who placed their hopes on Kaiser Frederick saw in the Chancellor the greatest supporter of reaction. Those who expected everything from the Crown Prince, more from personal than political reasons, regarded Bismarck as the most decided impediment in the way of the realization of their plans. Even at this stage there were germs of those intrigues which we shall refer to again later.

It is useless to speculate as to how things would have developed had Kaiser Frederick lived to realize his political hopes. On the whole, he appears to have aimed at a gradual change of German administrative and social life in a democratic direction. But it is unnecessary to state that in such a task he would have encountered enormous difficulties, considering the state of things in Germany at that time. Then came death—on June 15, 1888—and set its inexorable seal on all.

The memoirs of the Empress Frederick, which are still awaiting publication, will some day reveal to the world what she and her husband strove for during those many years, and what were the plans that had to be laid aside for ever, without hope of resurrection in the man who succeeded to the throne.

CHAPTER III

THE YOUNG RULER

Four months before his accession, when he was still only Prince William, speaking at a banquet given in honour of representatives of the province of Brandenburg, the future Kaiser protested most energetically against those bellicose descriptions of himself that were current both at home and abroad.

"I am well aware," he said, "that the public at large—particularly in foreign countries—credits me with ambitious and warlike thoughts. May God keep me from such criminal folly! . . . Yet, gentlemen, I am a soldier."

This little speech is reminiscent of the well-known "Prologue" in the classic tragedies. In the Prologue strange contradictions are indicated which lead up to and foreshadow the inevitable climax. Here was a young, untried man, who already looked upon himself as a misjudged individual, and who was fully determined to convince the world that he was better than his reputation. "Yet, gentlemen, I am a soldier."

In European diplomatic circles there was both uncertainty and anxiety at the time of the new Kaiser's accession, and the leading articles in the principal newspapers of the world—outside Germany—show the same feeling. Even if he did not become a disturber of the peace in the literal sense, there was a very strong possibility that he might bring into international politics an element of restlessness that was likely to create apprehension. It was, therefore, a comfort to know that old Bismarck stood at the helm, and that on account of "the deep, almost passionate admiration which the young Kaiser felt for him, he was likely to enjoy unlimited authority for some considerable time at least."

But there were some who knew that this was a mistaken supposition. The Kaiser and his Chancellor would only work together for a short time, and then some fine morning his Majesty's "hasty temperament and military zeal" would result in Bismarck's dismissal.

These characteristics revealed themselves in a remarkable way at the very moment Kaiser Frederick expired. Hardly had the Royal Standard on the castle of Sans Souci been lowered in token of what had taken place, when troops, who had been awaiting orders, came hastening from all sides as if to an assault, and guarded all the gates. The whole of the palace, park, and courtyard resembled a fortified camp. The result was that the most extraordinary rumours spread, and when at the same time several of the railway-stations on the lines leading to Sans Souci were occupied by considerable forces of secret police, these "conspicuous precautions," as the *Berliner Tageblatt* termed them, "gave rise to all kinds of disquieting comments." The whole thing was quite incomprehensible to the loyal citizens of Berlin, who had shown the most unmistakable tokens of sympathy with the Royal House in its grief.

On this very same day the new Kaiser again awakened surprise by issuing his two famous proclamations to the Army and the Navy, a breach of the tradition that first of all a monarch should always address himself to his whole people.

The first of these proclamations ran: " A firm, invincible devotion to the War-Lord is the inheritance of the Army, descending from father to son from generation to generation. Thus are we bound together, I and my Army. We were born for one another, and we will hold inseparably together whether God send us days of peace or strife."

In his proclamation to the Navy, after referring to the warm interest he had taken in it for many years, he concluded with phrases almost identical with the above: " We will hold together through good and evil days alike, through sunshine and through storm."

Three days later only he had a word to say to " My People "—that is, the Prussians. It was a proclamation in the style of a sovereign of the seventeenth or eighteenth century, in which he vowed to be " a just and merciful prince, to promote piety and the fear of God, to maintain peace, and to further the prosperity of the country." In contrast to the address made by his father, however, that of the young Kaiser did not contain a single political allusion, and it was not until his speech from the throne at the opening of the Reichstag that he disclosed any plans of government in the usual sense of the word.

"The German Kaiser's most important task," he said, "is to establish the political and military position of the Empire abroad, and secure strict obedience to the laws at home." In the sphere of home politics, he promised to continue the work of social legislation that his grandfather had inaugurated, and hoped that by those means he would be able to give to the poorer classes the help they needed in their struggle for existence. There is one passage which shows that Stoecker had not been his friend and companion in vain. All reforms were to be made "in conformity with the precepts of Christianity." It is true that some years later he came to the conclusion that "Christian Socialism is an absurdity, and that a priest least of all should hold such opinions," but as a matter of fact he has always worked in that direction, although with purely negative results.

Outwardly the Kaiser was the personification of a *pacifiste*.

"I am fully determined to keep peace with each and all," he said, "as long as it lies within my power to do so. My devotion to the German Army, and the position I hold in it, will never tempt me to forfeit the blessings of peace, unless war be forced upon us as a necessity by some attack upon our kingdom or our allies. Our Army will secure peace for us. It is far from my heart to wish to employ our strength in attacking others; Germany needs no more glory and no fresh conquests, now that once and for all she has won the right to exist as a free and independent nation."

He regarded Germany's alliance with Austria and Italy as a specially fortunate thing, for it would enable him to "cultivate personal friendship with the Tsar of Russia, and promote those friendly relations with the Russian Empire that have existed for a hundred years."

The members of the Reichstag were deeply impressed.

These remarks were inspired by his grandfather, who on his death-bed had bidden his grandson always to keep on good terms with the Tsar, and by Bismarck, whose policy tended uniformly in that direction. Therefore the applause was great when the Kaiser concluded his oration, and when he and Bismarck shook hands "the scene," in the words of a correspondent who was present, "made a deep impresssion upon the House, affording as it did a proof of the Kaiser's unchanged confidence in his Chancellor."

Three weeks later the Kaiser was at Kiel.

In a diary [1] of that time, under date July 14th, we have the historic information that for the first time a German King and Kaiser appeared in an Admiral's uniform when visiting his fleet. On the other hand, it only appears from the entries for the rest of the month that this visit to Kiel formed the starting-point of an official tour—the first of those many official tours which in the course of time the Kaiser was to make to the Courts of foreign potentates.

[1] In this diary, which embraces the years 1888–1908, and which was edited by the historian E. Schröder, *nach Hof-und anderen Berichten*, as the Editor says, the Kaiser has *gleichsam sich selber geschrieben*.

On this occasion the visit was to Russia, the initiative being from Berlin, as was repeatedly stated in the German Government Press. But the strained relations that had so long existed between Germany and Russia, and which at the beginning of the year 1888 threatened open rupture, showed no signs of relaxing. More than usual notice was taken of the fact that the official after-dinner speeches, at the family banquets at Peterhof, were not published either at the time or afterwards, and that the Russian Press exhibited no signs of joy or gratitude in connection with the visit. It was, indeed, more inclined to strike a note of irony, which grated upon the ears of Berlin. Needless to say, this did not pass unnoticed, and in an anything but friendly article the official *Norddeutsche allgemeine Zeitung* declared that the Russians were very much mistaken if they concluded from the visit that official circles in Berlin felt any greater desire for a better understanding between the two countries than was felt in St. Petersburg. " It is an exaggeration dictated by Asiatic ignorance and Asiatic pride."

But it was not enough to give a reply to Russia. France, too, must be made to understand that, notwithstanding all the Kaiser's peaceful intentions, Germany had no idea of showing any sentimental generosity. While unveiling a monument to his grandfather's nephew, the famous general Prince Frederick Charles, on the eighteenth anniversary of the battle of Mars-la-Tours, the Kaiser spoke out quite plainly. " I believe," he said, " that we of the 3rd Army Corps, and indeed the whole Army, know that there can be only one opinion on this point, namely that we would rather see our eighteen army corps and our whole population of forty-two million [1] men perish on the field of battle, than give up a single stone of what my grandfather and Prince Frederick Charles have won in fight."

This statement is worth remembering as the first example of that unconsidered, spontaneous eloquence which in the course of time has awakened so much comment both in Germany and elsewhere, and which has given diplomatists so many a troubled hour.

The Kaiser came back from his Russian tour, during which he had seized the opportunity of paying official visits to Stockholm and Copenhagen, as boisterous as a schoolboy after a good holiday.

He rushed at once to Friedrichsruhe to tell the Chancellor all about it. Bismarck was standing half dressed by his washbasin when the Kaiser, who had passed the night at Friedrichsruhe, walked into the Chancellor's bedroom in the early morning. Bismarck wanted to put on his uniform, but the Kaiser begged him not to take that trouble, and helped him into his dressing-gown.

It was an incomparable morning idyll with a touch of political artlessness about it, " as if," Bismarck said, " a young student who had no personal knowledge of people over thirty years of age should confess before an example of the species : ' This is the first old man I have found intelligent.' "

[1] In a previous speech the Kaiser estimated the number as forty-six millions.

THE YOUNG RULER

This description is a typical example of Bismarck's masterly talent in giving an impression, and its historic interest is increased by the circumstance that the little scene gives us a date upon which to base our decision as to the time when the intrigues against the Chancellor first began.

For the time being, however, the Kaiser had other things to think of than disposing of Bismarck. There were still many people to visit—the German Confederate Princes, the members of the Triple Alliance—to say nothing of England and Greece, where lived some of his nearest relatives. God only knew whether he could get it all into one year. Then there was the grand autumn parade of the Guards, a military spectacle with extensive manœuvres and marches, the whole thing lasting many days—presentations of colours, regimental lunches, shooting parties, baptisms of princes, review of the fleet at Wilhelmshaven, opening the free harbour at Hamburg, laying the foundation stone of the Law Courts at Leipzig, and the reception at Breslau of a deputation of Protestant and Catholic workmen's associations.

The diary shows how strenuously he worked. In August he had fourteen days engaged, in September fifteen, in October twenty. He paid official visits to Dresden, Munich, and Stuttgart, and did not forget that in his capacity of Prince in the German confederation he was a colleague of Prince Lippe Detmold, and went to visit him at his diminutive capital. During the same autumn he officially visited Vienna and Rome, and took the opportunity of seeing other parts of Austria and Italy.

The visit to Vienna was not entirely successful. He appeared to distribute arbitrarily from his stores of decorations, and created a somewhat painful impression by altogether omitting the Austrian Prime Minister, Count Taaffe, who, on account of his position, was entitled to a decoration as a matter of course. On the other hand, the Kaiser was a success in Italy. At a banquet in the Quirinal he reminded King Humbert that " our countries have both fought for their national unity, sword in hand, under the command of great leaders," and during a visit to the Vatican he had a long talk with that shrewd judge of men Pope Leo XIII, who no doubt made his silent observations.

Centuries had passed since Rome had been visited by an emperor, and the actual visit recalled the memory of the Middle Ages, and the German-Roman Empire with the same Emperor on both sides of the Alps. Rome was so delighted that it even tried to conceal its ruins with decorations of flags and streamers, and the new Cæsar's name was inscribed upon a marble tablet on the Capitol. The *via triumphalis*, however, went even farther. At Castellamare he witnessed the launching of the ironclad *Umberto,* and, in the company of the King of Italy, attended a naval review of more than forty battleships. At Naples he won the hearts of that colour-loving population, who, since the days of Joachim Murat, had not seen a sovereign with so many gorgeous uniforms. He changed from one to another : white cuirassier, black hussar, red hussar, general or admiral of the fleet. All about him rose a perfect tumult of cheering, and the royal phenomenon disappeared in a maze of colour.

A clever Italian journalist, who took service as a waiter on board the *Savoy*, tells us that the Kaiser simply overwhelmed his princely hosts. He persecuted the Prince of Naples—now King Victor Emanuel—by all kinds of practical jokes, and, for instance, squeezed his hand so hard under the table that the Prince could hardly conceal his pain. He made fun of the very high forehead of Signor Saint Bon—a member of the present Italian Government—and descanted with enthusiasm on Vesuvius, with its column of smoke rising straight upwards, "because," as Prince Henry said, "there is no wind." Finally he clinked glasses with Crispi, drained his glass, dashed it on the ground and looked smiling round the company.

A little later a flotilla of torpedo-boats passed by. The Kaiser was now on the bridge, and also the clever journalist. "Up to that moment," he says, "I had admired the Kaiser's versatile sprightliness, his infectious mirth, and warm-hearted manner ; but now I was struck by an indescribable expression on his face as he stood upright on the bridge, one hand resting on his sword, and the telescope held in the other. . . . There was no jesting then, no more laughter. The Kaiser was under the spell of two emotions : the beauty of the Bay of Naples and the splendour of the warships as they glided past. At that moment the artist in him was combined with the strategist, and it was impossible to say which of the two had the upper hand."

In Germany, however, where the official newspapers were conscientiously reporting all these occurrences, the public in general apparently failed to appreciate this extraordinary activity which was always on the move; for instead of eagerly following his movements on land and sea, or of enjoying details of parades and banquets, shooting parties and gala performances, naval reviews and manœuvres, the people were busy reading certain indiscreet revelations which had recently been published by Dr. Robert Geffcken in the *Deutsche Rundschau*, under the title of "Diaries of the Emperor Frederick." The authenticity of this work has never been contested, and its publication was undoubtedly the sensation of the year.

The Kaiser was what the Germans call *sittlich entrüstet*,[1] and in a speech to a deputation from the Berlin City Council, delivered immediately after his return from Italy, he gave his countrymen—and the inhabitants of Berlin in particular—a piece of his mind.

The City Council had decided to vote a sum of 500,000 marks for a charitable institution that was to bear the name of the Emperor Frederick, and in addition to erect a monument in his honour by public subscription. The latter in particular was an unusual form of homage, and in official circles it was actually regarded as an impertinence. The reception accorded to the deputation when it came with its double gift was therefore anything but encouraging.

"Here I am," the Kaiser said, "endangering

[1] Deeply insulted.

my health and exhausting all my powers in the effort to establish friendly relations and thereby further the peace and progress of my country and its capital, and the Press of my own capital, where I have my seat of residence, has dragged my family affairs before the public, and spoken of them in a way that no private citizen would suffer for one instant. . . . And especially I beg that in future you will refrain from quoting my father against me. It hurts me as a son most deeply, and is highly unbecoming in itself." He added, with an unmistakable indirect threat to Berlin: "Should I decide to reside at Berlin, I shall cherish the expectation that the Press will cease to discuss the private affairs of my family."

It is unnecessary to state that this extraordinary speech made a considerable sensation, and the effect of it was markedly increased by the Kaiser leaving the hall forthwith, neither shaking hands with the chief burgomaster nor allowing the members of the deputation to be presented to him. The German Conservatives made some party capital out of the incident, which they used in their campaign against the "Liberals," and the *Kölnische Zeitung* in particular was delighted at the manner in which the Kaiser on that occasion "had torn the mask from the Berlin Liberals in their patent leather boots." On the other hand, the Liberals knew quite well that it was precisely the semi-official newspapers which had been most eager to drag into public notice all the various details of the dissensions within the Royal Family respecting Kaiser Frederick's illness and the medical treatments employed. They therefore considered that it was perfectly unwarrantable of the Kaiser to vituperate the leading representative of the Liberal City Council, who had no part in the matter, and could not therefore be held responsible in any way for what was written in the Opposition Press.

The same views were expressed in a very sharp article by the *Times* correspondent at Vienna, who criticized in detail the short reign of the Kaiser. His opinion was that the latter's attitude towards foreign sovereigns and leading statesmen had been unfortunate throughout, and that the Imperial visits had served rather to create difficulties than to bridge them over. As far as the *Times* itself was concerned, it entertained no doubt " that certain aspects of the Kaiser's conduct are undoubtedly open to criticism . . . notably his treatment of Count Taaffe," but it also admits that " his popularity in his own country has not so far suffered any diminution."

In a kindly spirit judgment was reserved. The results, however, of all the Kaiser's efforts scarcely came up to the expectations they had raised. At the close of the year there was not one single European authority who ventured to assert that the diplomatic system which had created the Triple Alliance had gained any sign of fresh life, or that Germany had won a single new friend.

Yet whatever might be thought and said in Europe, the Kaiser still had Bismarck by his side.

" This thought suffuses me with joy and comfort," he writes to him in an autograph letter at the New Year. "I hope before God that for many years to come I may still be permitted to work beside you for the honour and advancement of the Fatherland."

CHAPTER IV

JOURNEYS AND INTRIGUES

THE Kaiser entered upon the New Year in the firm conviction that he had secured the peace of Europe for a long time to come. But the year 1889 showed many threatening clouds, and as he had still a number of visits to be paid, his course of action was plain. This was again " to risk his health and all his powers in order to secure new friendships," or, in other words, to set out on new journeys.

Owing to a number of circumstances, however, these journeys were considerably delayed. But after having fitted in during July the first of those many tours in Norway which during the following twenty-five years were to become an integral part of his annual programme, he did not delay one moment in following out the scheme of the preceding year.

This time he went to England, where he passed the first nine days of August. The visit was not official ; but its private character did not diminish the homage accorded to him both by the authorities and the general public. He was made an Admiral of the British Fleet, an honour which he retained till the outbreak of the Great War and which, according to his own words, he always valued very highly. In return he appointed his septuagenarian grandmother honorary Colonel of the First Regiment of Guards, and wired to Berlin ordering a detachment from the regiment to leave at once for England " to present itself before its royal chief." A few days later, in the company of the Duke of Cambridge, he was present at the manœuvres at Aldershot, in which 29,000 men took part. At the subsequent luncheon in the Duke's tent he made a speech couched in terms of the most unqualified admiration of the British Army. He reminded his audience of the British and German troops on the battlefields of Malplaquet and Waterloo, and in words which ought to be remembered to-day he said : " The British troops filled me with the highest admiration. If ever the worth of volunteers should be doubted, I shall be able to stand forth as a witness of their efficiency."

Two days later he embarked at Dover, reaching Berlin on August 11th. He was just able to make time for a single conversation with Bismarck on some important matters. On the following day he had to go to the Tiergarten railway-station to receive the Emperor Francis Joseph on his official visit, a return for the Kaiser's visit to Vienna the year before. At the State banquet the Kaiser in his speech reminded his guest of the Austro-German alliance and of the " gallant armies who are jointly responsible for the maintenance of the peace of Europe and who may have to fight shoulder to shoulder, if Providence should so ordain."

Another couple of days, and he accompanied his guest to the railway-station again; and after that for nearly two months he was touring through Baden, Alsace-Lorraine, Westphalia, Saxony, Hanover, Schwerin. He was present at an incredible number of manœuvres and parades, took part in sham fights and sieges, went stag-hunting, received deputations and torchlight processions, and delivered a long succession of official speeches on the standing theme of "the unity and greatness of Germany," listened to Wagner's "Meistersinger" and to the latest pattern of Mr. Edison's phonograph.

The Tsar's visit to Berlin on October 11th recalled him to the capital, where he had already spent a day or two between his various journeys. Judging from the Diary, the Imperial visit does not seem to have been particularly successful. Only three things are mentioned: arrival, shooting-party, departure. There is not a single other remark about either himself or his guest.

After having seen the Tsar off, he set out for Greece. His sister Sophia was about to be married to the Duke of Sparta—afterwards King Constantine of Greece, an event destined to have grave historical consequences. The old Empress Augusta, the Kaiser's grandmother, could not understand what was to be gained by this journey. In fact, her opinion was that her grandson travelled far too much, apart from the fact that this visit was sure to be too expensive to the Greek Court. But to the young Kaiser it evidently meant the realization of a beautiful dream.

"My first words to the Fatherland," he wires to Bismarck from Athens, " are a greeting to you from the city of Pericles and from the columns of the Parthenon. This magnificent vision has impressed me deeply." Further telegrams follow—from Constantinople and Corfu—for on this tour he made up his mind to pay a visit to the Sultan, a monarch whose capital used not to be included in the programme of Imperial visits. But the visit had a political aim, the inauguration of the German Balkan policy—the importance of which policy is being daily demonstrated in the Great War.

Abdul Hamid and William II became friends for life, and in a fresh telegram to Bismarck the Kaiser gave vent to his feelings in these terms : " After a visit which was like a dream, and which was made exquisite by the most magnificent hospitality on the part of the Sultan, I have just passed the Dardanelles in the most perfect weather."

In the Mediterranean he found an opportunity for another sensation. He detected a British squadron off Malta, and as he was a British Admiral, he seized the opportunity to inspect it. Hoisting his flag on the old battleship *Dreadnought*, he commanded as "Admiral for a day," beaming with joy over his title and his uniform. "One of the happiest days of my life," he called it in a speech some years later. The officers raged in silence, and the British Admiral prepared a report.

" Let him wear his uniform and his title, and let it stop at that, but don't let him come and worry us with his inspections," was the gist of it.

In Germany meanwhile the public was not much charmed with all these " private telegrams " which Bismarck did not cease to publish. Notably, the General Staff party, headed by Count Waldersee, was distinctly annoyed, and in the official Press articles appeared which bore witness to the general displeasure, and showed that there were forces already in motion to thwart the policy of the Imperial Chancellor.

Two days after the Kaiser's return Eugen Richter, spokesman of the Liberal Party, put a question to the Government on the matter. Herr Verdy du Vernois, who in his capacity of Minister of War had to defend the chief of the General Staff, performed this manœuvre with dexterity, and Count Herbert Bismarck, the Secretary for Foreign Affairs, was, of course, bound to assist him. For obvious reasons, however, there was no power in the defence. "It sounds like knocking on a tin plate," declared Bismarck's second son, "Bill," in a conversation with his brother. The expression, which is reminiscent of his father, strikes the nail on the head. But the Foreign Secretary was obliged henceforward to speak very often in the Reichstag, "and it was but seldom that his words had a genuine ring."

The Kaiser meantime had again escaped from Berlin, and while he was rushing from east to west on shooting-parties, visiting a succession of towns, being present at gala performances and parades, receiving deputations and inspecting barracks, the Berlin intrigues were winding themselves more and more tightly around Bismarck. The Chancellor was aware of them, but looked at the whole thing from its comic side. But the air was sultry and corruption was rife, and in the Memoirs of Prince Hohenlohe there is an atmosphere of intrigue and the baseness of small minds. The highest interests of the State were given over to chance.

The plot against Bismarck, which originally was worked by Stoecker, the Court chaplain, Hammerstein, the bribed Editor of the *Kreuzzeitung*, which subsequently became the anti-Bismarck organ, and Count Waldersee, can be traced back to the very first months after the accession of the new Kaiser. It was, at first, devoid of any political idea whatever, for the very simple reason that the brains which were scheming it had never produced a political thought or been able to approach public questions from any other point of view than that of private interest, either in connection with themselves or their friends.

Stoecker was the most conspicuous of the triumvirate, and his name will always be connected with one of the most remarkable periods in nineteenth-century Germany. He reached his zenith towards the end of the 'seventies, in the midst of the great economic collapse which was the natural result of the boom in speculations after the Franco-German War. It stands to his credit that he denounced the unbridled deification of capital which was the leading idea of the time; but he misunderstood the danger, and only recognized it in connection with the men " of the very black hair and the very high noses." His anti-Semitic feeling, which proved him to be a man with a narrow intellectual horizon, had gradually led him on to a wrong political track, and at the same time he attempted to create a Christian Socialist labour agitation, which necessarily brought him into collision with the Social Democrats. At that time, through dubious alliances, which were the result of contradictions in his own character, he found himself in a position where he ought never to have been, and it will always remain a stain upon his memory that he consented to work with men like Hammerstein and Count Waldersee. The former of these gentlemen revealed himself later on as a criminal of an elaborate type. His specialities—embezzlement, fraud, and chaffering with private letters from friends and colleagues— were in 1896 rewarded by seven years of imprisonment. The latter, whose military achievements we shall review in a later chapter, had not long since succeeded Moltke as chief of the General Staff—a burden too heavy for shoulders as slight as his.

At the moment, however, these men were in the height of Imperial favour, and with an audacity which would have been quite inconceivable but for that "student" spirit which Bismarck had noticed in the Kaiser, they had already fully prepared their plan of campaign. Thirteen days after the morning idyll in Bismarck's bedroom the *Vorwärts*, the leading organ of the Socialist Party, published a letter from Stoecker to Hammerstein. It contained the following sensational passage : "If the Kaiser notices that we are trying to breed discord between him and Bismarck, we shall certainly estrange him. If, however, we encourage his dissatisfaction over the things where he is in agreement with us, we shall be strengthening him on the main points without goading him. He said quite recently, 'I will give the Old Man six months to breathe in; then I will rule myself.'[1] We must therefore, without giving up any of our hopes, move with caution."

It is not surprising that after the publication of this letter Stoecker was so compromised that he had shortly to resign his position as Court chaplain. What is more surprising is that Hammerstein was able to remain in favour for a number of years longer.

As far as facts are concerned, in these intrigues against Bismarck, this letter is not, after all, so damning as it looks at the first glance. It was no news that forces were at work for the overthrow of the Imperial Chancellor, and even if the Kaiser had uttered the words which Stoecker imputed to him, and the authenticity of which has never been doubted, there was no positive proof of duplicity in his conduct. Yet Stoecker was right when he warned his friends to be prudent; for it is a maxim in psychological experience that impulsive natures are very often those which have to be approached in the most roundabout way if they are to be brought to a decision of real importance.

It is, therefore, rather difficult to pass a final sentence on the behaviour of the Kaiser towards Bismarck during the latter half of 1888 and the

[1] In the original: *Sechs Monaten lang will Ich noch den Alten verschnauffen lassen; dann regiere Ich selbst.*

whole of 1889. The only thing which can be positively asserted is that the Kaiser was vacillating on the question of whether he ought to part with the Chancellor or not. At the same time, he was deeply impressed by his mighty personality and his extraordinary services to the Fatherland, and, when carried away by these impressions, he let himself express strong feeling, the sincerity of which at the moment there is no reason to doubt.

His letter to Bismarck on New Year's Eve 1888 has not a false note in it, and in January 1889 even Hohenlohe was convinced that " the Kaiser is entirely under the influence of Bismarck, and that he has not even as much confidence in himself as to venture to express a view differing from that of the Chancellor."

In the course of the spring and the summer, however, difficulties of various kinds gradually came up.

During a disagreement with Switzerland concerning the expatriation of a German police-officer bearing the cheerful name of Wohlgemüth,[1] the attitude of Bismarck, in the opinion of many people, was needlessly rigid. No one was more troubled at this line of conduct on the part of the Chancellor than the Grand Duke of Baden, the uncle of the Kaiser. His chief claim to immortality was based upon the fact that at the proclamation in the Gallery of Mirrors at Versailles he had proposed the first official cheer to the first German Emperor. Therefore he could not look on calmly at the blunders of Bismarck, which might compromise the safety of the realm.

[1] Mr. Cheery.

"All our plans of war are based upon a friendly neutrality on the part of Switzerland," he declared. "A possible breach with that country might end by throwing it into the arms of France and thereby expose our left flank. The Kaiser," he said, "ought to step in with his Imperial veto to re-establish good relations with the Swiss republic, even if an action like this should result in the resignation of the Chancellor." Besides, Bismarck was far too yielding in his policy towards Russia, and, on the other hand, as far as Austria was concerned, he was of opinion that in a possible conflict between Austria and Russia, Germany's wisest plan on the whole would be to remain a passive spectator.

On August 24, 1889, writes Hohenlohe in his Diary, a conflict had arisen between the Kaiser and the Chancellor, and the Grand Duke of Baden considered it wiser to face the possibility of Bismarck one day taking his departure.

"And what will happen then?" Hohenlohe asks. "The Kaiser probably thinks he can direct our foreign policy himself. But that would be a very dangerous plan."

But all the prophecies were falsified, just in the same way as the prophecies of an imminent war with France and Russia. Bismarck would not agree, and in spite of all the passing thunder-clouds, he continued to enjoy the full confidence of the Kaiser. In particular, the Emperor was immensely pleased at the energy the Chancellor exhibited in pushing the Old Age and Disablement Insurance Bill through the Reichstag.

The Chancellor succeeded, and on New Year's

Eve 1889 the Kaiser felt once again an irresistible desire to thank him, just as he had done twelve months before.

"I know very well," he wrote, "how much of this success is due to your self-sacrifice and your creative energy, and I pray to God that for many years to come He may grant me the benefit of your tried and faithful counsel in my heavy and responsible position."

CHAPTER V

THE BREACH WITH BISMARCK

TEN weeks later there was nothing left of the Imperial New Year's prayer.

The Diary gives us some few facts on which to base a judgment on this rapid metamorphosis, the most important being a conversation on February 1, 1890, between the Kaiser and General von Caprivi, Commander of the 10th Army Corps, who was destined to become Bismarck's successor. But we look in vain in the Diary for any psychological explanation of the change ; nor is such to be found in the Memoirs of Prince Hohenlohe, notwithstanding the many important details that they give.

It was said in Berlin that Bismarck had become very irritable and changeable of late ; he laboured over trifles, constantly changed his views, and indulged in uncontrolled expressions about the Kaiser in conversation with foreign diplomatists. What was worse, however, was that the Kaiser suspected him of conducting secret foreign negotiations tending to a rupture of the Triple Alliance and to a *rapprochement* with Russia—a thing the Kaiser would never agree to. Then there was that difference of view on social legislation which cleft them apart at the very moment when the Kaiser had determined to appear before the world as an international reformer.

"Trifles every one of them," declared the Grand Duke of Baden, who had lately been on very intimate terms with the Kaiser. The real reason of the rupture was simply a question of power. "Are we to have the Bismarck dynasty or the Hohenzollern dynasty to reign over us?"

A week after the dismissal of Bismarck, Prince Hohenlohe paid him a visit, and expressed his unqualified astonishment at what had happened.

"It took me entirely by surprise," he said.

"That was the case with me also," replied Bismarck. "Even three weeks ago I did not think that it would end like this. But I was bound to expect it, sooner or later. The Kaiser intends to govern by himself."

These words give us the key to the Kaiser's rupture with Bismarck, and thereby save us the trouble of setting up hypotheses and drawing conclusions. The rupture was neither the result of any accidental question of the day, nor did it proceed from difference of age; still less was it a historical necessity. It was founded simply and solely on the personality of the Kaiser, with its typical qualities—unbounded love of power, guided by unalterable faith in his own perfection.

During the twenty months which had passed since his accession to the throne, his mind filled with ambitious dreams and autocratic ideals, the Kaiser had attracted attention to himself on many occasions both at home and abroad. His main characteristics were even then patent to all the

THE BREACH WITH BISMARCK 55

world—they did not lie very deep—and the future had nothing to add to them. His natural atmosphere was sensation. He lived and breathed in it, thanks to his changeful disposition, his tireless energy, his radiant self-confidence. The society in which he had grown up, and to which he was deeply attached, was exactly suited to foster all these qualities. Here was no political background, no parliamentary traditions, no earnest democracy imbued with a love of honour and strong in determination. On the contrary, there was a most regrettable abundance of all those servile qualities which Treitschke, the famous historian, about the middle of the nineteenth century had summed up in the word *Bedientengesinnung*,[1] and which the Germany of to-day has baptized with the suggestive name of *Byzantinismus*.[2]

But deep down in the national soul, independent of all political and social occurrences, there remained an element of sound sense, which had to be dealt with cautiously, for in the long run it would not let itself be defied with impunity.

Kein Schein verführt sein sicheres Gefühl,[3]

runs a famous line in Schiller's "Wilhelm Tell." It was this golden truth which Bismarck and the old Emperor never forgot in their dealings with the German people. Even at this moment, when the weaknesses of their system are far more

[1] Literally: a functionary or servant-like conception of life; a community steeped in official views and sentiments.
[2] After the Byzantine Empire, the classic ground of servile flattery.
[3] No appearances can deceive its sure judgment.

conspicuous than in their own times, this truth remains practically unshaken. Bismarck deprived the German nation of all power at a cross-road in its history, took the work of unification, which was in a fair way towards completion, out of its hands, and finished it according to his own mind. But in this very fact there was an undeniable proof of the purposefulness of his work which should claim, at least from his contemporaries and their nearest descendants, some pardon for his high-handed action. William II, who within the space of a few months leaped from the position of a comparatively insignificant prince to the dignity of German Emperor—a change which might have disturbed a better balanced nature than his—was very likely, just because of his temperament and all his theories, to make serious mistakes, especially at the beginning.

Nevertheless, the nation would have been patient with him, quite instinctively, if it could have seen any attempts at self-criticism, any serious efforts to study political situations in their relations of cause and effect, and to learn from them. Instead of this he was touring about the world within a month of his father's death. This was a new form of foreign policy, at which the nation looked with wonder not unmixed with distrust, and it is a fact that this feeling grew rather than diminished during his constantly repeated visits to the same Courts, with their wearisome series of return visits. But it would appear that right up to the outbreak of the Great War he remained convinced that by these visits he was fulfilling a mission of peace of the highest value.

THE BREACH WITH BISMARCK 57

The sincerity of this feeling is as incontestable as the inability to realize facts which has always characterized his policy, and which sooner or later was bound to lead to disaster. The word "difficult" has never existed for him except as a figure of speech, and one of his biographers most truly observes that "the Kaiser has always believed that he could reconcile deep historical antagonisms by kissing his dynastic guests on both cheeks."

It goes without saying that Bismarck, who had known the Kaiser since he was a boy, and who had observed the many strange developments of his complicated nature, entertained no illusions as to remaining in power till the day of his death, and this is confirmed by one of his speeches in the Reichstag. This speech also completely demolishes the theory that he ever intended "to found a dynasty." Speaking in the Reichstag in 1889, he most positively denied any such intention, stating in plain words that the thing a man least of all can bequeath to others is that confidence and experience he has gained from his personality and his work. That his power rested on a tottering foundation he knew well, and he drew attention to this, not once only but many times, before it gave way altogether.

Even more convincing in this respect, however, is the fact that Bismarck, by frequent absences from the capital and by protracted visits at Friedrichsruhe, actually tried to adapt himself to the Kaiser's eagerness to be free and unrestricted, and thus to pave the way for his own exit without any breach. Home politics did not interest him very much, and he was far from considering himself indispensable in this department. But his attitude was very different with regard to foreign policy, which needed the guidance of a firm hand lest even the work of unification should be jeopardized, and naturally he felt a distinct anxiety about handing it over to others unless he was to have the strongest guarantees in return.

It was, in fact, on this question that the first dissensions arose between the Chancellor and the Kaiser. Bismarck, as we have seen, had throughout a long life constantly aimed at maintaining good relations with Russia, with a single exception in 1878, when he considered that Russia was "suffering from a surfeit," and that it was necessary, on both political and philanthropic grounds, that Europe should "obtain relief for her."

The Congress of Berlin, which was appointed to carry out this drastic treatment of Russia, performed its task with a thoroughness which left nothing to be desired, and of which we see the consequences in the present situation in the Balkan Peninsula. Russia returned from Berlin gaunt and shrunken, but only six years later, in 1884, Bismarck was successful in concluding a secret treaty with her. This treaty, which is known by the very expressive name of the Reassurance Treaty, was not particularly attractive from a moral point of view, but in its political aspect it was something of a masterpiece, especially as long as the treaty concluded between Germany and Austria in 1879 [1] was kept secret also.

By the treaty with Austria Bismarck protected

[1] The basis of the present alliance between the two countries.

THE BREACH WITH BISMARCK 59

himself against Russia. By the treaty with Russia he protected himself against Austria. In this fashion he deceived both of them, and secured the benevolent neutrality of both in the event of an attack on Germany by France. It is true that this position was somewhat weakened in 1887 by the publication of the treaty [1] with Austria, but this very fact made it increasingly important that the treaty with Russia should be maintained.

The Kaiser held a contrary opinion. He did not wish the treaty to be renewed, but this by no means amounts to saying that he desired to pick a quarrel with his great neighbour. On the contrary, he had already decided to pay him another visit in the course of the year. Bismarck, who knew the Tsar,[2] and was aware that this good-humoured bear did not particularly enjoy over-frequent official embraces, tried with all his power to dissuade the Emperor from paying this visit. But with his unbounded confidence in "the fascinating strength" of his own personality, the Kaiser of course resented the advice of Bismarck.

It was left to the future to reveal which of the two was right. Within a year after the Kaiser's second visit to Russia the Franco-Russian alliance was an accomplished fact.

In the field of social legislation, Bismarck had gone so far in meeting the wishes of the Kaiser as to resign his presidency of the Board of Trade in favour of Herr Berlepsch, who was the mouth-

[1] The chief contents of it were published in Bismarck's well-known organ *Hamburger Nachrichten* in 1896—six years after it was annulled.

Alexander III. (1881–94).

piece of the Imperial views in the Government. Bismarck, however, had laboured so long on social questions, both in theory and practice, and had reaped so many bitter experiences of the vitality and fighting spirit of Social Democracy, that he did not feel much reassured by the Imperial declaration: "Leave Social Democracy to me! I can soon deal with that!"

Another example of the "student" attitude, an attitude in which it is impossible to rule a State.

"My young master is ardent and full of life," wrote Bismarck some years later, referring to events in the winter and spring of 1890. "He wishes to make all men happy. At his age this is natural. I myself doubt the possibility, and I have told him so.... It is quite easy to exert an influence over him if you suggest thoughts and plans which he thinks will make people happy. He can hardly wait one moment before putting them into execution." Therefore Bismarck felt a certain hesitation about the Kaiser's new social policy—politics are not so simple, after all, as chemical combinations—and in order to neutralize the effect of these reforming tendencies of the Kaiser, he persuaded him into the scheme of an International Labour Conference.

The Kaiser, who has always had a notable gift for seizing the ideas of others and shaping them according to his fancy, was enthusiastic over the notion. Here was an opportunity for reforming social legislation, not only in Germany but in all the States "whose industries rule the world's markets together with our own," to quote a passage from the Imperial Rescript concerning the

THE BREACH WITH BISMARCK 61

Conference. He was no more only the " Peace Kaiser " ; he was the " Workers' Kaiser," an even more beautiful title. But from that moment Bismarck felt easy as to the result of the Conference. The whole thing would come to nothing. And such was indeed the fact.

The first official announcement of the International Labour Conference was issued on February 4, 1890, three days after the Kaiser's conversation with Caprivi. At a meeting in the Reichstag five years later, Herr von Berlepsch, in the name of the Kaiser, gave a brief report of various details in connection with Bismarck's resignation ; he also mentioned the first political conversation between the Kaiser and General von Caprivi.

" I have summoned you here," said the Kaiser, " to tell you that you must prepare for all contingencies. Sooner or later the Imperial Chancellorship will be vacant. I have selected you to be the successor of Bismarck. My grandfather had already selected you for this office—in the event of Bismarck's death. But things look now as though I may have to part with him earlier." The Kaiser turned out to be a true prophet. The differences of opinion between him and Bismarck in the department of both home and foreign policy were too great to admit of their working together any longer—apart from the fact that influential persons were constantly trying to prejudice the Kaiser by disparaging remarks about Bismarck. They represented him, not only as a man who was obstructing the political rights and authority of the Kaiser, but even went so far as to suggest that the Chancellor was a confirmed victim of the morphia habit.

The Kaiser asked Professor Schweninger, Bismarck's physician-in-ordinary, and received an answer which had " both horns and teeth," to use Luther's expressive words.

" It is a miserable calumny, and I know the source of it," replied the Professor.

But by degrees the ground was undermined beneath the Imperial Chancellor's feet, and at last there came the inevitable crash—brought about, as always happens, by something utterly different from the question at issue.

As early as 1889 some of the Ministers, without the knowledge or consent of Bismarck, had begun to take the liberty of dealing directly with the Kaiser and obtaining his signature to important documents, the contents of which were only made known to Bismarck when they could not possibly be altered. The Imperial Chancellor had accordingly reminded his Ministers of the Cabinet Order of 1852. By this order, which was still in force, all important affairs had first to be laid before the Prime Minister—whose duties were now absorbed in those of the Chancellor—and by him to be reported to his Majesty. Bismarck, in his official resignation, enlarged upon the importance of this Cabinet Order, and it is an irony of fate that the man who had entered public life in contempt of everything like ministerial responsibility, and who had ruled in this spirit for twenty-eight consecutive years, should be overthrown just when trying to uphold this principle against the new autocracy which was beginning to raise its head.

THE BREACH WITH BISMARCK 63

"*Summa lex regis voluntas*," declared the Kaiser in conversation with a Conservative member of the Reichstag.

These words, which are quoted from the most ancient of German Constitutions, the famous *Golden Bull*, are clear enough. As this document, however, dates from 1356, the political views expressed in it could hardly be described as particularly applicable in 1890. At the request of Herr Bleichröder, the famous banker, Bismarck consented to have a conference on March 14th with his old opponent, Herr Windhorst, the parliamentary leader of the Centre. The conference, which did not lead to any result as far as home policy was concerned, has become historical, owing to the fact of its being immediately reported to the Kaiser by some benevolent person.

At that moment the bomb exploded.

Early in the morning of March 15th the Kaiser called at Wilhelmstrasse, at the office of Herbert Bismarck, and ordered the Imperial Chancellor to report himself at once.

Bismarck, in his later years, was no early riser; he was stiff in body and limbs, needing massage and special baths to retain his vigour in any degree.

But that morning there was no indulgence—no good-humoured Kaiser to help him put on his dressing-gown. The Chancellor had to struggle into his uniform and hasten before his master. Still, he had not forgotten the words of Mephistopheles about the "formidableness" of youth. The scene struck him as having a distinctly comic side, and later, when talking to Harden, he compared his position to that of Hamlet's murdered father, who was summoned away without time for preparation: —

> ... disappointed ...
> No reckoning made, but sent to my account
> With all my imperfections on my head.

His Majesty demanded, in an excited tone, that the Chancellor should cease to confer with any of the party leaders without his knowledge.

Bismarck declared that he could not give up that liberty, and that he could not easily place himself under control with respect to the persons with whom he had intercourse.

"Not even if your master orders you?" asked the Kaiser.

"My master's power ceases at the door of my wife's drawing-room."

After this dangerous beginning the conversation turned upon the Cabinet Order of 1852. The Kaiser demanded that it should be repealed at once. Bismarck protested, declaring that his position would become quite untenable if, in the first place, he were not permitted to control his own Ministers, and, in the second, were prevented from conferring with those members of the Reichstag whom he wished to see.

The breach was irreparable, and three days later —March 18, 1890—Bismarck sent in his resignation. On the preceding day he held his last conference with the members of the Government and informed them of what had taken place. Now comes the most astonishing part of this very painful episode—namely, the Kaiser's reply. "With deep emotion," he says in this document, which is dated

THE BREACH WITH BISMARCK

March 20th, " I see from your resignation of the 18th inst. that you have decided to retire from the office which for many years you have occupied with such notably successful results. I had hoped that the question of parting from you would not have arisen as long as we both remained alive. . . . The reasons you adduce for your decision convince me, however, that any attempts on my part to induce you to withdraw your resignation are not likely to be crowned with success." As a special sign of his favour he created him Duke of Lauenburg and presented him with a full-sized portrait of himself, thanking him at the same time in the most profuse manner for all his services to Kaiser and Fatherland. " God bless you, my dear Prince, and may He grant you during many years to come a cloudless old age, bright with the consciousness of duty faithfully discharged."

The time has not yet arrived to pronounce a final judgment on this document, but it is easy to understand why it never made much impression, either by its matter or manner, upon the contemporaries of the Kaiser, especially considering all that we now know with regard to Bismarck's resignation. It is difficult to reconcile the Imperial conviction of the hopelessness of prevailing upon Bismarck to remain in office with the fact that it was the Kaiser himself who precipitated his resignation, and that on March 17th—the day before he tendered it—the Imperial Chancellor received two several messages instructing him to hasten.

A few days later the Kaiser sent his famous telegram to the Grand Duke of Weimar. This is also one of the historical documents connected with Bismarck's resignation, and at the same time a valuable *document humain,* throwing a light on its Imperial author:—

"My heart aches as though for the second time I had lost my grandfather. But this trial has been sent me from God, and therefore I have to bear it even if I should be crushed by it. To me has fallen the post of officer of the watch upon the ship of State. We shall keep the old course; and now—full steam ahead!"

CHAPTER VI

THE NEW MASTER

MEN would have to be less easily impressed than they are if William II had not overwhelmed them by breaking with Bismarck.

His unsuspecting contemporaries who concerned themselves only with the purely external aspect of the event stood lost in admiration before such a powerful display of energy and will. There was something attractively bold in this young man who, after governing for twenty months, could dispense with every kind of guardianship, and without hesitation take the helm of the State into his own hands, at the same moment that he invited the whole world to Berlin to solve the social enigma.

When had any one seen a young Emperor so brave, so resolute, so dominated by great ideas?

There were only a few who shook their heads and remembered Goethe's words :—

"Die Botschaft" hör ich wohl, allein mir fehlt der Glaube.[1]

But it was not so very long before it became apparent that it was just those few who were right.

[1] I hear the message, but I lack the faith.

The truth of the matter is, that the breach with Bismarck, far from being the outcome of any very remarkable qualities in William II, was, on the contrary, prompted by the weaknesses in his character. All the dilettante element in his nature, which was fostered by flattering and unreliable friends, now came triumphantly to the front with his belief in his own perfection.

"We shall keep the old course—full steam ahead!"

If the great bulk of his contemporaries, and particularly of his own countrymen, had possessed the power of reflection, they would at once have become aware of the hopelessness of this paradox.

Bismarck could not be set on one side after governing for twenty-eight years, and yet the course remain as before. This man represented a system —independent of the fact that he himself was a personality. Endowed with an appreciation of the truth, untouched by any mysticism or sense of theatrical effect, he realized that even "blood and iron" had their limits, and, based on this sober conviction, he tried to conduct a consistent foreign policy, the leading idea of which was concentration. For the sake of this policy he not only laboured to maintain friendly relations with Russia, but he even conquered his instinctive dislike of England, and as late as the year before his retirement he realized that any policy that might endanger the traditional good understanding between England and Germany would be fatal. "Even if we were successful in building a fleet as strong as England's we have still to fear an alliance

THE NEW MASTER

between England and France. This is a policy that we cannot continue."

It was just this old course that William II discarded at the moment when he " dropped the pilot," and it is only one more proof of his imperfectly developed political capacities and the want of forethought in all his actions that he came forward with no further intention than that of simply taking the tiller into his own hands.

Fortunately, the majority of his countrymen had more foresight than himself.

" We Germans are superior to others in every direction," said a Prussian statesman some years ago to Prince Bülow, who was Chancellor at the time. " But there is one thing in which we are lacking."

" What is that? " asked the Chancellor, who himself refers to the conversation in his well-known book, " Deutsche Politik." [1]

" We are perfect asses in politics."

Never was this so apparent as at the moment when Bismarck retired. Everything that could be called public criticism died, not only the power of political reflection, but also the faculty of seeing what was most important in the most powerful mind of the nation.

" One would think that courage, veracity, and every recollection of Germany's greatness had disappeared from German soil," says the well-known political author Otto Mittelstädt. The base and despicable attitude which the German Press took up, before the eyes of the whole world, towards

[1] A volume of the work " Deutschland unter Kaiser William II," translated into English under the title of " Imperial Germany."

Bismarck in disgrace cannot be fathomed by any measure of contempt.

Hohenlohe also felt that all was not as it should be. As early as March 24th he notes that there was an overwhelming sense of complacency in Court circles. People went about as "jolly as sandboys" because they could now talk openly, and no longer need be in fear of the great man. In the Reichstag Bismarck's retirement was not mentioned at all, but on the other hand he was enthusiastically cheered by the people as he drove to the station as a "Lieutenant-General of Cavalry," with a military escort, on his way to Friedrichsruhe. But this demonstration had no real significance; it was only a spontaneous outburst, without a trace of the indignation which alone would have been worthy of the moment.

It is against this strangely unsympathetic background that we must consider the change of system which was now introduced. It is the beginning of the age of $\epsilon\pi\iota\gamma\text{ον}\eta$,[1] all that intensely modern, materialistic Germany with its overwhelming discipline, its progressive efficiency, its ubiquity, and all the amazing results of these things; but at the same time with its crushing of all personality, its love of official phrases, and its State-made morality—*Deutschland über Alles*, as unavoidable in theory as in fact.

Hohenlohe notices the change after three months.

"Two things struck me during the three days I was in Berlin," he says in his Diary for June 18th. "The first is, that no one ever has any

[1] Increase or growth.

time to spare, and that there is much more bustle
than before. The second is that all individuals
are puffed up. Every one is conscious of himself.
Those who were formerly suppressed under the
overwhelming influence of Count Bismarck have
now all expanded like sponges soaked in water.
This has its advantages, but it also has its dangers.
There is no unity of feeling here."

At the moment, however, all promised well.

The International Labour Congress, which the
Kaiser had summoned in response to Bismarck's
pessimistic suggestion, opened on March 15th, the
same day on which the historic encounter took
place between the Emperor and the Chancellor.
The Minister of Commerce opened the Congress
with a speech in the name of the Kaiser. His
Majesty did not appear at the opening, as many
of his people had expected, neither did he attend
a single one of the meetings. To make up for
this the members of the Congress were invited
to a great Court reception and concert, at which
the Prince of Wales and his son, the present
King George, were among the guests. There was
also a banquet at which the Kaiser presided.
In a conversation with the well-known French
politician Jules Simon, who later on published
an account of this *tête-à-tête*, the Emperor appeared
as a *grand charmeur*, and seems to have entirely
captured this benevolent, highly cultivated, but not
particularly keen-sighted judge of human nature.

The Kaiser's French is excellent, and his knowledge of French literature simply bewildering. He
has his likes and dislikes, and hides neither the one
nor the other. Zola arouses his displeasure : " He

poisons the public with immorality, and by no means deserves his popularity. But Georges Ohnet is another man altogether—an author of whom France may be proud."

From literature they passed rapidly on to social questions, and from these to military ones. Jules Simon frankly brought forward the question of war between France and Germany, whilst emphasizing that love of peace which is ingrained in the French nation.

The Kaiser became animated.

"I tell you plainly. Your Army has worked well. If, therefore—which seems to me impossible—you took the field against the German Army, no one could predict the result of such a fight! Therefore I regard the man who would drive these two nations into war as a criminal and a fool."

But of course the Prince of Wales was not forgotten either.

At a banquet given on March 22nd the Kaiser appeared in the uniform of an English Admiral. In his speech he reminded the Prince that their nations were brothers in arms at Waterloo, and he expressed the hope that the British Fleet, in conjunction with the German Army, might prove strong enough to maintain the peace of the whole world.

Old Moltke, who was sitting near, turned quickly to his neighbour, Prince Hohenlohe, and reminded him of Goethe's words: "A political song is a poor song." [1] He also expressed the hope that the Imperial speech would not get into the news-

[1] The original text: "Ein politisch Lied ein garstig Lied."

papers. But everybody was not so wise as the old Field-Marshal. The next day the "Waterloo speech" was repeated all over the world, to the astonishment of the general public, who could not understand the object of it just when the French delegates to the Labour Conference were staying in Berlin.

This criticism, which, of course, was perfectly justifiable, shows, however, that the Emperor was not understood. One cannot expect to find any consistency in a nature such as his beyond the purely military and monarchical ideals which had become a part of himself, and were of vital importance to his own power. In everything else he lived and breathed in an atmosphere of caprice. His presents were just as astonishing as his words, and at the conclusion of the Labour Conference he sent Jules Simon a folio edition of Frederick the Great's musical works, beautifully bound, and with an inscription in the Kaiser's own hand.

A few days later he went to Bremen and laid the foundation stone of a monument to his grandfather. The event was interesting—not in itself, but because it was the Emperor's first public appearance after the retirement of Bismarck. He spoke at the Town Hall and also on board one of the North German Lloyd's steamers. Although his meaning was a little obscure, it was clear enough to show the principles which guided his government right up to the outbreak of the Great War.

"It is a tradition in our house," said he in a speech on the part played by the Hohenzollerns in the development of Germany, "that we regard

ourselves as chosen by God to govern and guide
the people over whom we are appointed to rule,
so that we may promote their welfare and further
their material and spiritual interests. . . . Whatever clouds or dark days may be in store for our
Fatherland, our Navy, or our commerce, surely
we Germans shall nevertheless succeed by vigorous
striving towards the goal in accordance with the
good maxim, ' We Germans fear God, and nothing
else in the world.' Therefore I will make this
request to you. Should much of what appears in
the Press and in public life seem obscure to you,
and should—as unfortunately happens far too often
—my words and utterances have all sorts of mean-
ings ascribed to them which are not justified,
remember what I actually said, and remember
also that old maxim of an old Emperor, ' The
word of an Emperor must not be twisted or turned
about.' " [1]

As a hymn in praise of absolute power, this
speech is perhaps one of the most typical he
has ever made. The German nation is here invited
to commit itself to him without criticism, in the
firm confidence that he has not only the will
but the power to guide everything towards the
highest good of the Fatherland. He is to lead
the way in political, social, and economic matters,
furnish the inspiration for agriculture and commerce, mechanics and navigation, literature and
art, ethics and science. Besides all this, he as
supreme War-Lord, must keep the Army and
Navy on a level with the times, and by continual

[1] Rudolf of Habsburg (1273–90), founder of the present
Imperial House of Austria.

THE NEW MASTER

travelling on land and sea forward the interests of European peace.

But it is not enough to obtain the submission of adults only. Above all things it is necessary to instil those ideas into the young from their earliest years. A common foundation of discipline, loyalty, and the fear of God must be laid, which shall coincide with the official system to be defended. Every person must thoroughly understand that patriotism and the Hohenzollern cult are identical, that criticism is evil, and that "those who oppose me I will strike down."[1] Every single German must go out into life as a missionary for this idea, instil its principles at home and abroad, and carry it as a banner before him into all parts of the world.

The Kaiser still took his stand on the same ground as Bismarck, that the Germany which had been created as a result of united effort had enough problems to solve in Europe, and that its worldly ambitions ought not to extend farther than to take part in the peaceful international competition which consists in raising intellectual and material standards, and creating new conditions for civilization and progress. But in practice this aim was already becoming too narrow for him.

One step more and he was in the midst of his projected task, that of making Germany a World-Power, with all the possibilities involved in such a policy. Involuntarily he felt the necessity of making some reservations, and in this same speech we are

[1] Original: diejenigen welche sich mir entgegenstellen zerschmettere ich.

considering he said: "Moments may occur when doubts may be felt in the business community, and when it may seem to the uninitiated as though things were approaching a crisis. They may be quite sure, however, that many things are not as bad as they appear to be."

But there was one class which refused consistently to follow the lead of William II, and this class was supported in the Reichstag by an increasing number of voters.

The year before, while receiving a deputation of miners, the Kaiser had referred to the socialistic Labour Movement in these words: "To me a Social Democrat is synonymous with an enemy to the Empire and the Fatherland," and that speech naturally produced its effect. At the Reichstag elections in 1890, in the midst of the Imperial endeavours to guide the Labour Movement into the official path of loyalty and confidence in the vigilance of Government, the Social Democrats secured 1,400,000 votes. It was an answer which could not be misunderstood, and in a speech made to a commission appointed that same year, to reform the higher educational department, the Kaiser emphasized the necessity of exterminating Socialism by means, among other things, of public education. "All the vague and confused reformers of the world who are constantly turning up, are to a large extent a product of this higher education, with its unreal and defective system, which serves only to turn out an academical proletariat. All these so-called famine candidates—that is to say the gentlemen of the journalist profession—are in numerous cases starving students. It is

THE NEW MASTER

dangerous. This over-production must be checked. My ancestors held their fingers on the pulse of time, and were able to foresee the future course of events. Consequently they kept themselves at the head of the movement which they had determined to guide and lead on to the new goal. I believe that I have rightly understood what are the tendencies of the new spirit, and the century now drawing to its close, and I am resolved, in the matter of the education of our coming generation, to open up new ground, as I resolved in the matter of social reform."

There is an excess of confidence underlying these words which would be impressive if they expressed a really unbiassed attitude in the face of past and present events. Now they were only a further revelation of the two most conspicuous weaknesses in the Kaiser—his lack of historical comprehension and his displeasure, not to say his exasperation, at anything in the nature of free criticism.

No one who is acquainted with the history of the Hohenzollerns will seriously allege that they ever " held their fingers on the pulse of time and foresaw the future course of events." The truth is that there were a number of distinctly second-rate persons among them, and that many of them, who were somewhat bombastic, shrink considerably on closer examination. Some of the best of them, among whom was the old Emperor William, were forced to take the steps most beneficial to the country by bold and far-seeing counsellors. The Kaiser knows nothing of this. To him every Hohenzollern is a Christian, a hero, a warrior, with great plans and high ideals. As their descendant, he will lead the way for his people and for the whole world in the struggle for human civilization.

But distrust is deeply ingrained in human nature —even among the Germans. "A spirit of disobedience is creeping over the country," he says in the speech at the beginning of 1891. "Wrapped in a bright and deceptive garment, it is endeavouring to confuse the minds of my people, and to lead astray the men who are devoted to me. It expends an ocean of printer's ink and paper to conceal those paths which are as clear as daylight and which must be clear to every man who knows me and my principles. But I will not allow this to trouble me, though it should cut me to the heart to see my intentions so misconstrued. Our present party divisions are founded on interests which are often pursued far too keenly, each man for himself. It is greatly to the credit of my ancestors that they never stooped to serve political parties, but always kept above them, and that they were successful in uniting the various parties in work for the good of all."

This assertion also betrays a regrettable confusion of ideas, which can only be the result of a faulty teaching of history in youth. He was, by teachers whom he had reason to consider high-principled and sincere, gradually led to adopt an historical view quite inconsistent with fact, and we have heard that his most distinguished professor at Bonn was horrified at his pupil's attitude with respect to history. With his vivid imagination, his restless, domineering will, and his antiquated ideals, he became from the time of his accession an easy prey to that faithless *coterie* which, with Waldersee as leader and Philip Eulenburg as his most dangerous satellite, fostered all the fantastic illusions and arrogance in his nature. This circumstance must be considered as a certain excuse for William II, and at the same time as an explanation, not only of Bismarck's fall but also of the fate which later on overtook Caprivi —to mention two of the most characteristic examples. But in reality these two episodes were only part of the natural introduction to that domination the further course of which is displayed so remorselessly to-day—the whole series of attempts and half-measures, blunders and disappointments, dramatic victories and political defeats, which characterize the government of William II right down to the outbreak of the Great War.

He is the young Emperor in the second part of "Faust," risen from the dead at the end of the nineteenth century.

> Ihm ist die Brust von hohem Willen voll,
> Doch was er will, es darf's kein Mensch ergründen
> Was er den Treusten in das Ohr geraunt,
> Es ist gethan, und alle Welt erstaunt.[1]

It is therefore quite consistent that the system of government by surprise, which was now introduced, and which for years to come was to give

---

[1] His mind is with a lofty purpose full;
Into his purpose though must no man enter.
What to his trustiest he softly breathes,
'Tis done,—and all the world with wonder seethes.

the world so much to talk and write about, should be inaugurated by an historical play which was a glorification of the greatest event of the year.

Six months after Bismarck's fall a play was put on the stage at one of the Berlin theatres with the significant title *der neue Herr*. As a dramatic work it was utterly worthless, but the subject of which it treated had an immediate interest, which showed that the author was a good man of business. It told how the " Great Elector " —the Kaiser's historical ideal—when a young man had managed to get rid of an inconvenient Minister.

"Everything depends on the way one makes the King look at things,"[1] says one of the characters in Lessing's *Minna von Barnhelm*.

In this case also the truth of this remark was proved.

The Kaiser saw the piece several times, applauded it in a demonstrative manner, and distinguished not only the author but also the principal actors.

His action, however, was not a well-considered one.

The public, though they did not fathom the nature and extent of all that was involved in the downfall of Bismarck, and had been tranquil witnesses of his dismissal, felt on further consideration that they were by no means particularly charmed at seeing the episode displayed upon the stage.

[1] Original : Tout dépend de la manière dont on fait envisager les choses au roi.

CHAPTER VII

AN ENLIGHTENED POLICY

FOUR days after Bismarck's dismissal and the appointment of Caprivi the old and the new Chancellors took breakfast together. Bismarck, who had not yet moved out of the Chancellor's palace, wished to ask his successor to the house in order to show him that he personally bore no ill will to him, and Caprivi, who had no pettiness in his nature, accepted the invitation in the same spirit.

It was inevitable, however, that feeling should be a little strained.

"I feel like a small child, with its eyes bound, who has been pushed into a dark room," Caprivi confided to his hostess, Frau Johanna. During the meal he remarked to Bismarck :—

"If the Kaiser sent me and my army corps to a place where we were threatened with destruction, I would first remonstrate ; but on the command being repeated, I should obey without inquiring what the result might be. I shall do the same thing in my present position."

This utterance gives us an admirable insight into Caprivi's loyal character ; but at the same time it throws a glaring light over the system which could misuse such a character in so Oriental a manner. It was docility now, and not skill, which was the most important quality in a Chancellor.

A few days later Bismarck took leave of Caprivi in his writing-room.

"Has your Excellency anything to tell me or any question you wish to ask?" said the retiring Chancellor, with the right which his genius and his fifty years' experience of public life gave him, in such a moment as this.

"I have nothing to tell your Highness nor any question to ask your Highness," answered the new Chancellor, who had not yet been a week in his position.

This answer, which in no way expressed Caprivi's personal opinion, was a compulsory one. At the audience on February 1st, when he had made representations to the Kaiser and referred to his complete ignorance of State matters, with which he had never had anything to do, his Majesty had calmed him with a sovereign assurance :—

"Never mind! You will receive all your instructions from me."

Thus did Caprivi, at the age of fifty-nine, enter upon the highest and most responsible office in the State, without a single link with the past and without a single conference with Bismarck as to the main lines of his home and foreign policy. It constituted such a complete breach of everything which is known as continuity in public life that it is not easy to find a parallel to it in recent times.

But it is not sufficient for a sovereign who has

AN ENLIGHTENED POLICY

determined to act for himself to have docile Ministers with just enough intelligence to grasp his ideas and defend his views in the National Assembly. He must also himself speak directly to the nation, to give them directions and wise advice. As long as the old Emperor lived the German people had not been much indulged in this respect. William I, like all the Hohenzollerns [1] until the time of the present Emperor, with the single exception of Frederick William IV, was a man of few words, and the things he had at heart he instructed Bismark to communicate to the Reichstag. With William II there came a decided change. It attracted attention at first, as anything new will do, but comparatively soon lost its effect through constant repetition. Even at the time of Bismarck's fall a reaction had already begun to appear in public opinion as to the continual speeches and the continual journeys. Yet this was just the moment when he wished to establish himself definitely as the tireless missionary of his people both at home and abroad.

The scanty notes in the Diary, unmarked by a single critical remark or shadow of reflection, are an indication of the rush and hurry which characterized his restless existence. Impressions speed by like glimpses of a landscape seen from the window of a railway carriage. During the first three months after he had taken the tiller of the State into his own hands he was engaged on forty-eight days in the capital and out of it. He laid

---

[1] Neither the Great Elector nor Frederick II—to mention the two most conspicuous representatives of the family—have left behind them a single recorded speech.

foundation-stones of churches and quays, inspected garrisons, took the lead in parades and in siege manœuvres, was present at sacred concerts and at baptisms, and even found time to become acquainted with the latest improvements in instantaneous photography. He went to see his grandmother, Queen Victoria, at Darmstadt; the Empress Elizabeth of Austria, yearning for solitude, was honoured by a visit from him in Wiesbaden. A few days later he stayed the night at Wartburg, and slept in the room with that historic stain on the wall left by the inkpot which Luther flung at the devil.

The opening of the Reichstag recalled him to Berlin, and in his speech from the throne he announced that he was determined to meet any revolutionary attempt to shake the existing order of things " with inflexible determination." At the same time, he announced as a fact that " I have been successful with all foreign Governments in establishing the trustworthiness of my policy." He remembered both the living and the dead—including Moltke's services in peace and war (which he suddenly took a fancy to remind him of in a telegram), General Pape's sixty years' jubilee as an officer, the hundred and fiftieth anniversary of Frederick II's accession to the throne, and the four hundredth anniversary of the birth of Duke Albrecht of Prussia.

There was the echo of a sigh in the words he pronounced when unveiling a memorial to his grandfather at Wernigerode, in Saxony: " All rulers have their troubles, and from time to time they feel the need of rest." But this was only

AN ENLIGHTENED POLICY

a passing weakness against which he himself is a living protest. The next day he was in Essen, far away in Western Germany, where he made a speech to a deputation of 750 of Krupp's workmen, while twenty-four hours later he dedicated a number of new banners at Lichterfeld, near Berlin.

Ten days later he was at Christiania—the beginning of a foreign tour which lasted two months, and included, among other things, a fresh official visit to England and the second of those official visits to Russia to which Bismarck was so much opposed. At a banquet at the palace of King Oscar he gave a frank explanation of his reason for so many journeys. " I consider it necessary for a ruler," he said, " to gain his own information about everything and to collect opinions from their direct sources and to learn to know his neighbours so as to create and maintain good relations with them. These are the objects of my journeys abroad."

There is no reason to believe that these words were not meant exactly as they were spoken. But it is beyond doubt that life and circumstances have given them quite another scope than that of satisfying a natural desire for knowledge, and the desirability of cultivating acquaintanceships. By repeating these journeys year after year they gradually became part of a political and economic system, the object of which was to open the way for German wares, German methods, German capital, German culture and ideas. In this way a certain unofficial, but none the less important, co-operation gradually established itself between the monarch, who was constantly conveying his speeches, and his uniforms, about a continent, and the ordinary commercial traveller with his samples and his trunks. Each wanted to " gain information " for himself and " to maintain good relations with others." German capital followed all over Europe, new enterprises sprang up, especially after the problem of transmitting electricity over long distances had been solved. German engineering triumphed, German chemical industries no less. German mechanics ran up their scaffoldings in all countries, while architects built German habitations to the best of their ability, so that the strangers might feel themselves at home. It was a display of natural powers, determined ability, and antlike industry which it would be foolish not to recognize as a whole, and as foolish to deny the Germans their right to be proud of. The dangerous side of it was that it contained an element of exaggeration, which might easily become importunity, in a people like the Germans, whose sensitiveness is so poorly developed and who are so markedly unable to understand the ideas of others.

It was in this way that by degrees the German *Weltpolitik* [1] arose, which, from its very nature must be aggressive, and of which the Kaiser, with his impulsive temperament, his military and autocratic ideals, his self-confidence, and his underestimation of all difficulties, seemed to be a specially fitting exponent. His speeches, particularly those after 1895, teem with illuminating information on this point, whilst the years imme-

[1] World policy.

diately following Bismarck's fall—or, in other words, the period we have now reached—may be considered as an introduction to it. There was, therefore, a certain domestic character about Caprivi's Chancellorship. There was time to pay attention to home affairs, and also to combat Bismarck publicly and to plot against him, with the assistance of Ambassadors abroad. In spite of all the official journeys, or, more truly, because of their exaggerated frequency, a certain instability was observable in foreign policy, whilst the colonial policy, towards which Caprivi never had any inclination, gradually became characterized by a degree of pedantry and pomp which for years to come made that branch of German administration more or less of a caricature.

One of the main reasons for Bismarck's retirement was, as we have seen, his disagreement with the Kaiser in respect of the Reassurance Treaty with Russia. To the Kaiser, and therefore also to Caprivi, this treaty did not seem entirely loyal to Austria-Hungary, an opinion which no one is likely to dispute; but, on the other hand, it was evident that the link with Russia could not be abandoned without closer ties being formed in some other quarter. Only one State could be thought of in this connection—namely, England. There was no greater admirer of her sea power than the Kaiser, whose naval schemes at that time were still in their embryonic stage and whose ambition went no farther than to have the largest and the most perfect of armies.

The most evident sign at that moment that England and Germany were drawing together was the so-called Heligoland Agreement of June 17, 1890. In that agreement, which took the form of an exchange, England ceded the island of Heligoland to Germany. In return Germany gave up the Protectorate of Witu and Somaliland in East Africa, just north of the British possessions, and also the Protectorate of Zanzibar and the neighbouring island of Pemba, which, however, Germany had never actually possessed. Owing to the great importance of this island to her, England decided, both on practical grounds and as a matter of fairness, to come to an amicable agreement with the Sultan of Zanzibar on payment of a sum of money.

Opinion upon this agreement coincided in England and Germany, though the standpoints were different. As an expression of British public opinion, a remark by H. M. Stanley was much quoted. "Heligoland for East Africa and Zanzibar—it is like exchanging a trouser button for a whole suit," said the well-known explorer, who was undoubtedly qualified to give his opinion on the subject.

The Germans looked at it in the same way. That glittering "trouser button," the use of which they could not then understand, aroused their anger, and it would be easy to prove by quotations from articles in the Press to what a height the tide of their displeasure and bitterness was running at that time. Many of the opinions then expressed were based on misconceptions which time has long since dispelled; others have proved themselves remarkably persistent right down to recent years, and were not actually silenced until the

AN ENLIGHTENED POLICY

outbreak of the Great War. This is no proof, however, that the Kaiser was in the right and the people in the wrong at that time. Rather should it be said that this displeasure was grounded upon a real and true popular instinct, which such an impulsive nature as the Kaiser's could not grasp. German colonial rule in Africa had been founded by pioneers, whose work had attracted attention in the Fatherland, and raised justifiable hopes which had now to be abandoned, without the nation getting any satisfactory explanation of the reason for such a policy.

In Hohenlohe's Diary for June 19, 1890, there is an interesting but not very correct piece of information, to the effect that the Heligoland Agreement was an act of necessity on Germany's part because the latter, through her colonial policy, had "trodden on England's corns" to such a degree that there was a danger of an alliance being formed between England, France, and Russia if some satisfactory arrangement were not reached at once. It is much more likely that the agreement was the natural outcome of a policy which "lived from hand to mouth " in the belief that one bird in the hand—even the most miserable fledgling sparrow—is worth ten in the bush. The Kaiser had visited this island, as he tells us in one of his speeches, when he was fourteen, and ever since then he had wished that one day it might come back to the German Empire. Now the opportunity had come. The inhabitants of Heligoland were bound by language, customs, and interests to their kinsmen on the mainland, and, " thanks to the beneficent wisdom of the Government under which you have been until now, no changes have been forced upon you during the time you have formed part of the mighty British Empire." This quotation, which is taken from the Imperial proclamation to the people of Heligoland on August 10, 1890, is a fresh evidence of that freedom from prejudice which is such a characteristic feature of British world policy, and which at that moment suited the Kaiser exactly. "I incorporate this island as the last piece of soil in the German Fatherland without strife and without bloodshed," he said to the marines who paraded on the occasion. "This island is destined to be a bulwark against the sea, a protection to German fishermen, a base for my warships, a defence for the German Ocean against every enemy who may force his way in and attempt to show himself there."

In these words lies the whole of the Kaiser's Heligoland policy—the desires of the past and the programme of the future. In this matter he showed more foresight than the majority of his countrymen, owing to those naval schemes which he had not yet thought fit to mention in his after-dinner speeches, and which could have obtained no hearing in Germany at the time—schemes the aim of which was to have a sea-going fleet equal in every respect to that of the British.

The recovery of Heligoland was the greatest event of the year 1890, and, upon the whole, the most significant occurrence during the reign of William II until the outbreak of the Great War. On the other hand, as a political move it was an absolute failure, and contributed particularly to

AN ENLIGHTENED POLICY

make bad blood with Russia. From the Diary, the Russian visit would seem to have been very successful. At Narva the Kaiser visited a large factory close to a waterfall, which was illuminated with Bengal fire and electric light. In Memel he was greeted by jubilations and peals of bells. He came home laden with gifts—a magnificently bound album containing photographs of Narva, a Bible dated 1649, a troika team of three splendid horses, and a whole armful of knitted gloves made by the Lithuanian women. This list is a good illustration of his favourite expression, " Nothing human is alien to me." On the other hand, the political results of the journey were very poor. A few brief toasts were exchanged in French, and as soon as the Kaiser had left the Russian newspapers hastened to assure the public that relations between Germany and Russia were exactly the same as before the visit, and that there was not the slightest change in Russia's attitude towards France.

In the following year the French Fleet visited Kronstadt, and the conclusion of the Dual Alliance between the Republic and the Empire of the Tsar showed beyond all doubt the true value of all this enlightened policy, with its Bengal fire and electric light. The results of this policy disappeared at the very moment when the Imperial special train crossed the German frontier.

The people of Germany went through the same experience after their Emperor's first official visit to England in the summer of 1891. The Kaiser hardly ever exerted himself more to make a good impression than he did on this occasion. For nearly a week he was engaged from early morning onwards with a perfectly stupendous programme. He received numerous addresses and deputations—the only exception being the deputation from the British and Foreign Association for Arbitration between Nations, for which there was no time left. He was present at luncheons, gala performances, and banquets; he conferred with leading politicians, held countless reviews, changed from one uniform into another—up to the number of five in one day. To put it shortly, there was not a point of etiquette which he did not observe with the greatest conscientiousness, and, moreover, with a certain pride in showing that all these things were mere trifles to him.

He was up at seven in the morning, and while the Court was resting from the fatiguing programme of the day before, he went for a refreshing ride in Rotten Row, and returned with renewed strength ready to start work again.

His greatest day was the one when, as London's guest, he was welcomed at the Guildhall by the Lord Mayor, with all that mediæval ceremony which the City, in a spirit of admirable self-respect and piety, has continued down to the present day.

The Lord Mayor presented the Kaiser with an official address of welcome, enclosed in a beautiful casket ornamented with jewels. On the lid there were views of the City, with an allegorical design in the centre, which latter, unfortunately, was worthy neither of the time nor the occasion. It represented the City of London surrounded by German eagles—an ominous kind of prophecy which the Zeppelins of the future were to illustrate in a strange fashion. The Kaiser was overwhelmed.

His shrewd old grandmother, who knew her impetuous grandson, had foreseen that moment, and as she was afraid that the Franco-Russian Alliance, just then in the honeymoon of impetuous warmth, would be too much for his feelings, she had, after conferring with Lord Salisbury, desired to see beforehand the speech which the Kaiser proposed to make at the Guildhall. After a number of alterations and expurgations, which were official secrets at the time, and which kept the wires between Berlin and London busily employed, a quite unimpeachable form had ultimately been found.

This labour was not in vain. Never had the Kaiser spoken in a more dignified manner or with so little declamation as on this occasion. The speech was entirely free from the usual military nonsense, and his wishes and plans for peace were untainted by any hankering after political alliances. " My aim is, above all, the maintenance of peace. For it is peace alone that can give that confidence which is necessary for the healthy development of science, art, and trade. . . . I shall always be found ready to unite with you and with others in our common labours for peaceful advancement, friendly intercourse, and the progress of civilization."

In spite of all this, the German mind proved but a barren soil in which to cultivate the belief that Imperial journeys were a certain means of securing European peace. It was not long either before the sound sense of the nation found its natural expression. The pompous Imperial hymn, "Heil dir im Sieger Kranz," had become worn by frequent repetition. The text needed renewing, and one day the following rhyme was heard in Berlin: —

> Heil dir im Sonderzug
> Reisest noch nicht genug;
> Reis immer mehr.[1]

Some good moral lies at the root of most popular rhymes, and in comparing the present with the past the regret of the people rose almost bitterly to the significant conclusion of the verse: —

> Weun du dann bald entgleist,
> Rasch du zum Bismarck eilst
> Holst ihn uns her.[1]

---

[1] In the *Contemporary Review*, vol. 62 (1892), the above verse is rendered thus in English :—

> All hail to thee! In special train
> Still travel on and on again;
> When soon you do run off the rail,
> You'll hurry off to Bismarck then
> And we shall welcome him again.

CHAPTER VIII

POLITICAL CHESS

THE people of Germany had reason to feel a certain bitterness. They had looked on, *kühl bis ans Herz hinein* [1]—to quote one of their contemporary newspapers—while Bismarck was turned out of office, in the ingenuous belief that " the course " would be the same as before, if not entirely so in the field of home politics, which interested them only moderately—still at any rate, in regard to relations abroad. The nation did not know, and could not know, anything of the Russo-German Reassurance Treaty of 1884, which the Kaiser had decided to drop. But they saw the consequences of this policy in the demonstrative conclusion of an alliance between France and Russia. On the other hand, the Heligoland Agreement had not led to any noticeable improvement in their relations with England, whilst it was a painful fact that their hopes and expectations with regard to their African colonies were now considerably diminished. But, above all, the nation saw—and this contributed more than anything else to arouse discontent—that Bismarck had been treated in a manner, and this by those in the highest quarters,

[1] Cool to the very core of the heart.

which was utterly unworthy of the Government of a great nation, and which cast a slur upon it. It has long been admitted that Bismarck's attitude towards the Imperial Government, in the years immediately following his retirement, was far from unimpeachable ; but, on the other hand, it is only fair to state that from the very beginning he had been subjected to a system of petty annoyance which would have been unthinkable in any other civilized country. It is interesting to note that this system received its severest condemnation from William II himself, when he frankly admitted several years later that he—the Emperor—was under a complete delusion at that time. But as long as it was possible to practise them, these annoyances were practised in his name and formed a typical illustration of this new period of absolute power when the many ruled—exactly as they did in the days of the ancient autocracies.

We have mentioned Hohenlohe's impression of the feeling in leading circles during the months following Bismarck's fall. It was the basest informers and flatterers who now abused the Imperial confidence and sowed suspicions in that impetuous nature, which was as jealous of its honour as Othello. They used their time with a perseverance which was worthy of a nobler end, and barely eight weeks after Bismarck's dismissal a circular, bearing Caprivi's signature, but naturally with the Kaiser's knowledge and approval, was dispatched to the German ambassadors abroad. In this document Bismarck was directly accused of carrying on a policy which he knew to be jeopardizing, at least in part, the true interests of his country.

POLITICAL CHESS

The Imperial Government, which "discriminated between Bismarck as he was and as he is," tried to avoid everything which could contribute to "darken in the German people's mind the picture of their greatest statesman," but at the same time they expressed the hope—which the ambassadors would naturally endeavour to fulfil—"that the Governments to which you are accredited will not attach any importance to observations in the Press with regard to Prince Bismarck's views on any subject."

When speaking to M. Herbette, the French Ambassador in Berlin, the Kaiser, some time later, expressed himself with a frankness which naturally made a great sensation:—

"The Duke of Lauenburg"—the Kaiser carefully avoided the historic name—"appears to be still very angry because I precipitated and accepted his resignation as Chancellor. I confess that it was extremely painful to me. . . . But what else could I do? Since then the Duke has given way to feelings which are quite unworthy of him. He has stepped down from that pedestal on which my own gratitude and that of the nation had placed him, and thrown himself over head and ears into an aimless and worthless agitation against me. . . . But do not suppose that I, as people assert, propose to secure by force, in the Supreme Court of the Empire, what the Duke will not give me willingly. No! The German Emperor will never show the world such a sad spectacle as that of bringing an action against that man in the days of his old age."

Thus were the fatal words uttered which

showed how perseveringly and unscrupulously the *entourage* of the Kaiser were carrying on their work. " Who can have encouraged, or indeed suggested, such ideas to the Kaiser?" asks one of his most thorough and most honest biographers with a certain dismay. The answer is ready to hand. No one but the "jolly sandboys."

But there was still an act to come in this lamentable drama. It was performed in June 1892, on the occasion of Herbert Bismarck's marriage with Countess Margarethe Hoyos, a member of the famous Hungarian family of that name. Bismarck had received information through his son that the Emperor Francis Joseph would give him an audience if he went to Vienna on the occasion of the wedding, and as he had decided to take part in this quite private family festival a notice was sent to the Press. And then the German Government became extremely active.

After having submitted the matter to His Majesty, Caprivi wrote a letter to the German Ambassador in Vienna which repudiated Bismarck in the most cutting words, and expressly stated that even if a reconciliation should take place between the Emperor William and Bismarck—in which the late Chancellor must naturally take the first step—it would never go so far as to justify public opinion in the belief that Prince Bismarck had earned the right to exert any influence whatever in the conduct of State affairs. Caprivi therefore requested the Ambassador, " in case Prince Bismarck or his family approach Your Excellency's house, to confine yourself strictly to the conventional forms of politeness, but to avoid any invitation to the wedding. This instruction applies also to the staff of the Embassy. . . . His Majesty does not intend to take any notice of the wedding."

This peculiar document, which was published in the *Reichsanzeiger* of July 17, 1892—about a month after the wedding, but of which Bismarck had already heard the nature during his stay in Vienna—attracted, as was indeed natural, painful attention. At the time of the Chancellor's fall, two years before, a French paper had informed Bismarck's countrymen that "the Germans are not a great nation." Many of them, in the light of subsequent events, admitted with grief and bitterness the justice of that verdict. But never was it so glaringly clear as now. It was petty tyranny in its worst form which now ruled public life from top to bottom, that spite and envy which Tacitus had noticed as one of the besetting sins of the old Teutons. But though rulers might wear themselves out *propter invidiam*—because of hate— there was in the character of the nation a tendency to hero-worship, and an element of affectionate gratitude which might be kept down for a time, but which could not in the long run be disregarded with impunity.

Now the measure was full.

At the moment when Bismarck, with the Kaiser's sanction, was officially entered on the list of those persons who were not to be received at an Embassy, and with whom people were warned to have nothing to do, while at the same time the semi-official press began to attack him in articles which intimated that he had undermined his own work, and that the harm which he had deliberately wished to bring on the Fatherland was incalculable, at that moment the German people rebelled. His journey back from Vienna resolved itself into a triumphal procession. In Dresden, Munich, and Kissingen the people surrounded him in enthusiastic crowds, and after his arrival in Friedrichsruhe, a perfect stream of processions marched out to do him honour.

This was such a direct expression of popular feeling that none of the representatives of " the new course " could remain in doubt as to how the land lay. But it need hardly be said that it never occurred to any of them to pay the slightest attention to it. The policy of journeys continued on its undisturbed way, with its speeches and processions, its flag-decked streets, and splendid illuminations. Either the Kaiser paid visits himself or he received visits in return, so that the nation, directly or indirectly, " almost unceasingly saw the eyes of the world directed towards the radiant façade of the State," to quote Harden. At the same time a lamentable confusion reigned in official life.

The Caprivian administration was in principle a kind of Liberalism, and with its Free Trade treaties, and its concessions to the Socialists and the Poles, there was really more Liberalism in it than in the Bismarckian policy. But its effects were naturally quite illusory, with a self-willed Emperor at the head of affairs, who was constantly in a hurry, and who therefore was exceedingly apt to interfere at unseasonable moments.

The policy of the Government was marked by contradictions and half-measures, and the views which were maintained by the Chancellor and by individual Ministers varied constantly, in sympathy with changes of opinion in the highest quarter, before the business in hand could be finally decided. The Elementary School Act was brought in and then recalled. The Army Act was passed at last with the narrowest possible majority, after it had first been rejected, in spite of the fact that, in presence of his generals at the New Year's Levée on January 1, 1893, the Kaiser had threatened to "smash the opposition to pieces." To put it shortly, official life in the Government and the National Assembly was dominated by a confusion which aroused misgivings, not only in the newspapers of the Opposition, and the extreme factions in the Reichstag, but also in quarters the loyalty of which was beyond all doubt. Involuntarily people asked themselves : " What does all this mean, and where are we drifting to? "

But the system could not be changed—or more truly, it had to be maintained, contrary to all sound and modern views, because a change would mean the abandonment of everything which the Kaiser, from his first accession to the throne, had constantly proclaimed as the highest political wisdom, and had made his goal and ideal as a ruler.

Then something happened which at one stroke created a new situation—at any rate, for a time.

In the summer of 1893 Bismarck became seriously ill at Kissingen. The Kaiser knew nothing of the illness until the danger was really over—a new proof of the way in which those who surrounded him tried to put Bismarck out of his memory; but instantly he realized what he ought to do. There was not the faintest idea in the Kaiser's mind of resorting again to Bismarck's advice, nor had he any political object in view, whereby to strengthen his own distinctly weakened popularity by reconciling himself to his old Chancellor. The whole thing was a spontaneous expression of kindly feeling, which does more credit to his heart than to his judgment. Therefore it was that his congratulatory telegram of September 19, 1893, to Bismarck, on the occasion of his recovery, aroused the greatest enthusiasm throughout the whole of Germany, and when Bismarck, in January 1894, visited Berlin, where he had not set foot for four years, not only he himself, but the Kaiser also, were the objects of unparalleled ovations. Through Bismarck he could reach the heart of the nation. It was only later on that the world came to know, by Hohenlohe's memoirs, that Bismarck's visit to Berlin was a work of necessity, since the Kaiser was resolved that he would not be the one to go to Friedrichsruhe. "Now they may build triumphal arches for him in Vienna and in Munich if they like," said he. "I am a head in front of him, nevertheless."

He gained no advantage, therefore, from his changed attitude towards Bismarck. Here—as in his relations with Caprivi and his colleagues—he was unable, from his lack of self-criticism, and from his unbounded love of power, to take any sensible advice. He had to do everything himself, and himself take the credit for everything that was done.

"I want the power; let those who wish keep the peacock feathers," said Cecil Rhodes once, with that strong, almost brutal directness which was characteristic of his creative genius. For the romantic William II power and peacock feathers have always been intimately connected.

Therefore it was not long before a coolness again existed between the Kaiser and Bismarck, and in spite of some Imperial advances during the last four years of the Chancellor's life, any real cordiality was henceforth out of the question.

One fine day the same thing exactly happened to Caprivi. He had—as we have already shown—taken upon himself the heavy task of Chancellor with the most self-sacrificing loyalty. He had subordinated his convictions and his power to the Imperial will, and placed his signature to official letters which would always stand as an accusation against him. But when, one day in October 1894, without further ceremony, he received his dismissal —not even accompanied by the words "released from office with assurances of royal favour"—he had not been compromised by sustaining any defeat in the Reichstag, nor had he undertaken anything in his official capacity which could have awakened the Kaiser's displeasure. On the contrary, in spite of his ignorance of the rocks and shoals of statecraft, he had manœuvred surprisingly well, and quite recently, in order not to arouse the Kaiser's disapprobation, he had himself assumed parliamentary responsibility for the so-called "Revolt Act," in the face of the Social Democrats, though in earlier days he had characterized the idea which underlay it as nearing the limit of political folly.

But he had forgotten to create a party for himself in the Reichstag or, which was of still greater importance, a party at the Court, which could quell the intrigues which were brewing. Therefore he was beaten by the more adroit Count Eulenburg, who, in spite of his poor abilities and want of character, made his way to the position of Prussian Minister of State, and subsequently wormed himself into diplomacy.

Eulenburg was, as Bismarck styled him, " a modern Cagliostro," forward and insinuating, " with a couple of eyes which would spoil the best breakfast for me." He himself has admitted that he felt ill at ease whenever he came across men of independent character, and that he preferred to meet them at a distance, in history, so as to avoid coming into personal contact with them. As a minor poet he possessed undoubted gifts, and with his extensive acquaintance with the terms of Greek and Scandinavian mythology, and of the German poetry of the Middle Ages, he could put into rhyme all the sentiments which the Kaiser was only able to express in prose. As a result of their artistic collaboration we have the " Poem to Ægir," written by Eulenburg, and set to music by the Kaiser—an event which, according to the Diary, the world became aware of on December 11, 1894.

As was remarked among other things by Herr Dernburg, the well-known Colonial Minister, it will always be somewhat of a psychological mystery how such a man as Eulenburg could retain the Imperial favour for so long; and when at last, after many years, William II turned him away,

POLITICAL CHESS

the effect on the country was immediate and salutary. But at this time he was a great man, whose plans might not be thwarted, and simply to stand in his path—even if Eulenburg carried the day—was enough to bring dismissal on the bold spirit who ventured on such a course.

This Caprivi was made to feel as no other had done; and with a loyalty which does him the greatest honour, he withdrew into private life without uttering a word in his own defence, the richer by numerous bitter experiences and a quantity of orders—among them that of the Black Eagle set in brilliants. He observed a strictly reserved attitude until his death, in 1899, and firmly refused to have any memoirs whatever published, notwithstanding pressing requests from highly influential quarters.

The dismissal of Caprivi was such a sensational event that the echo of it rang through Europe, and with an audacity which could hardly be more defiant, the *Kreuzzeitung* wrote the following comment on it: "The wind which blows the mighty from their seats now changes much too rapidly. It is possible to go peacefully to bed with a vote of confidence to-day, and early to-morrow morning be drummed up by Herr von Lucanus[1] with a request to prepare one's resignation."

There was no exaggeration in this. The ship of State had long ago been left to the mercy of chance, and it went full steam ahead—on a zigzag course.

---

[1] Privy Councillor at that time and the Kaiser's confidential adviser.

CHAPTER IX

THE JUBILEE YEAR

IN 1895 the German Empire celebrated its great jubilee year.

A quarter of a century had passed since that important period in the history of Europe which is marked by the fall of the French Empire and the foundation of the unity of Germany. It was an event which was calculated to appeal in a special degree to national sympathies, and to awaken memories which were dear to every German. The crown of victory had indeed suffered at the hand of time, and many leaves which had shone golden once were now pale under the merciless searchlight of history. But there were still thousands living of those who had taken their part in 1870, who remembered their losses and wounds, their happiness and the proudest moment in their lives, which had come to them in the fight for the restoration of the Fatherland ; and there was reason to expect an outburst of national feeling which would re-echo through the world.

Nothing of the kind took place. The jubilee year, considered as a festival, was almost a fiasco. The working classes showed an indifference and a suppressed irritation which was the natural consequence of the many mortifications to which they had been subjected—not to mention that the "blood and iron" policy, which was now celebrating its greatest anniversary, was so essentially different from that of the Social Democrats, that nothing could bridge the chasm. The propertied classes were divided by conflicting interests. The air was heavy with painful scandals, and in politics incapacity sat enthroned in the person of the seventy-five-year-old Chancellor, Prince Chlodwig zu Hohenlohe Schillingsfürst, whom the Kaiser, with a sense of humour which might have been excusable if it had not referred to the highest and most responsible Minister in the State, had christened by the name of "Uncle Chlodwig." But neither was there any widespread want of loyalty, in the first place, because the nation was not enough developed in political respects, and secondly, because it clung to the belief that the Kaiser's intentions were for the best. There was merely a steadily growing doubt as to his power to realize these intentions in practice.

All this is sufficient to explain the lack of force in the Kaiser's speeches. His words march up in rigid file : "God and our German sword," "allegiance to the colours," "fidelity towards the royal house," "blind and unconditional obedience," "the laurels of victory," "the bloody field of honour "—a long procession of phrases extending through months of festivities. There was not a single new thought in them, not a seed with power to grow and teach something to the coming generation. To the nation the events of 1870 were the result of work and devotion to duty through long years in combination with the best of those qualities which had distinguished the moral and intellectual life of their country, and which were still of service in the peaceful competition of everyday life. To the Kaiser the jubilee year was "a great festival of thanks and a commemoration of the great Emperor of blessed memory"—as he himself expressed it.

It was therefore unavoidable that sharp discords should break in upon the festive joys.

On the twenty-fifth anniversary of Sedan the Kaiser stigmatized the Social Democrats as "a gang of men not worthy to bear the name of Germans," and called to the representatives of his Army, that if the nation would not disassociate themselves from these men, "you must arm yourselves against the traitorous crew, and lead a campaign which shall rid us of such creatures."

On another festive occasion he said: "The more people fall back upon catchwords and party considerations, the more firmly and surely do I reckon on the fact that my Army—be it at home or abroad—will stand ready to obey my wishes and my signal." And with an intention not to be misunderstood, he reminded them of his grandfather's words of greeting, in 1848, to the officers who welcomed him back after his banishment: "These are the gentlemen whom I can trust."

The whole failure of the jubilee year lies dismally exposed in these expressive words. Here stood the Emperor at the moment when he wished to inaugurate the *Weltpolitik*, which was the natural continuation of the struggle for unity inaugurated twenty-five years before. As a means of embody-

THE JUBILEE YEAR

ing this policy he had a Navy which—to use his own words—"certainly is small to look at," but which, nevertheless, was "stronger than other navies on account of its discipline and the unconditional obedience towards superior officers which it shows."

William II, since he was a boy, had taken an exceptional interest in everything concerning the Navy. His first ideal, as a creator of a German fleet, was the same man who was his ideal in so many other things—the Great Elector. Here was a tradition to build upon, and one which appealed to energies latent in the nation. These only needed to be aroused in the right way. The revolutionary poet Freiligrath had appealed to them before the middle of the century, and with the well-known phrase about "a future on the sea," which has been associated with the Kaiser since 1898, Freiligrath had already in 1848 proclaimed that

> ... in den Furchen die Colomb gezogen,
> geht Deutschlands Zukunft auf.[1]

But the Kaiser does not seem to have remembered these lines any more than he realized the peaceful trend of thought which underlies them. The German people, whose historic path had led them inland, as it were, for centuries, could by a steady hand be guided towards the ocean. In truth the first step had already been taken, through the development of a merchant fleet, which in-

[1] In the furrows which Columbus traced
Lies the future of Germany.

creased in size and importance from year to year. By the work begun during the reign of William I in the direction of establishing a national fleet, supported by a national shipbuilding industry, the necessary conditions had been established for a system of co-operation between the Navy and the merchant service, especially from the moment when Germany began to make an appearance as a colonial Power. It was unavoidable that a German colonial and naval policy which systematically aimed at advancing German interests beyond the seas should cross sooner or later the interests of the great colonizing Powers, and most of all those of England. The dissatisfaction which the public evinced with regard to the Heligoland agreement showed that the nation was willing to take the risks of this new policy, based on a fair recognition of the principle of open competition. Thus far the Kaiser could always count on having the nation with him. But certain conditions were absolutely necessary. The colonial and naval policy must be prepared with care, and developed in a far-seeing and unprejudiced manner—without fine phrases and without pedantry—and especially without too many complimentary allusions to the excellent qualities of the chief competitor.

Need it be said that not a single one of these essential conditions was fulfilled?

The Kaiser was not only devoid of any original ideas on naval affairs. He took, quite unconsciously, a perfectly irresistible delight in hammering this fact into the public mind whenever there was an opportunity. During the first seven years of his reign he paid a visit to England every single

THE JUBILEE YEAR

year, and received frequent visits in return. Every time he pronounced eulogies on England and the English Navy.

"Ever since our fleet has existed we have always exerted ourselves to form our ideas upon yours and to learn from you in every way. Our officers and men know the history of the British Fleet as well as you know it yourselves. The British Navy is for the German Navy not only a model of technical and scientific perfection, but its heroes too—Nelson, for instance, and others—have always been, and always will be, the guiding stars of German naval officers and men. Nelson's famous signal is no longer necessary. You Englishmen all do your duty, and we, as a young seafaring nation, come to England to learn something from the British Navy. Should it ever happen that the British and German Navies have to fight side by side against a common foe, then the famous signal, 'England expects that every man will do his duty,' which England's greatest naval hero sent out before the battle of Trafalgar, will find an echo in the patriotic heart of the German Navy."

But all this did not make the smallest difference—any more than the "Naval Cabinet" which he had established as soon as he succeeded to the throne, and the object of which was to secure for him the greatest possible direct influence in all things concerning the Navy. Several years later he founded the Imperial Shipbuilding League, where the details of all problems could be tested before being put in practice. The whole time he took an active share himself in the various questions which came under discussion. He followed the proceedings of the League, discussed questions of armour-plates and projectiles, the disposition of the guns on board battleships, questions of stability, etc., all with that ease which his natural versatility gave him, and with the authority attaching to his position. The really competent authorities whose lifework it had been to study these questions yielded to him when opinions differed, for it was naturally unwise to show him that he was mistaken, especially in the presence of a large assembly. The result was, as has been pointed out even by German authors, that at a time when the art of shipbuilding was developing at a tremendous rate all over the world, and distinguished chief engineers with original ideas were actively working in the great naivies, not a single talented shipbuilding engineer arose in Germany. All initiative died in the shadow of that rank omniscience. In the same fashion he wished to master everything technical and to exert his influential authority on materials and equipments, in spite of the Naval Department and the financial authority of the Reichstag. He also wished to have the human material under his control. At the beginning of his reign—he said in one of his speeches—he had found "a Navy whose excellent material in the way of officers and men did not fully realize that it was an absolutely necessary adjunct to the person of the Supreme War-Lord." But already during the jubilee year this state of things altered in a degree which caused him the highest satisfaction.

In speaking to his naval recruits he employed

a style of language which sounds more like the midnight monologue in "Faust" than a speech to young men. "The gracious God and I have heard your vow. . . . The vow is sacred, and sacred is the place where ye have sworn it. This is shown by the altar and the crucifix. It signifies that we Germans are Christians, and that we always begin by giving honour to God in all our undertakings. . . . Just as I, your Emperor and ruler, devote all my actions and aspirations to the Fatherland, so are ye also obliged to devote the whole of your lives to me. For ye have taken your oath as Christians. Ye are now at a time when there is a great demand for earnestness of service. . . . Remember then again that ye are Christians. Think of your parents—of your mothers, who taught you your first prayers."

But the fathers and mothers who sat at home from one year's end to the other were not inclined to take these exhortations too seriously when they read them in the paper. Affectation reigned supreme in Imperial naval affairs, and against this background of the vow, the altar, the crucifix, and the earnestness of service, some strange features developed.

But this was not all. The nation did not even know what new ships were in building. It heard the Kaiser complaining year in and year out that construction went on too slowly; but at the same time it heard—for instance, in 1891—about "the stately line of ships which compose our Navy," and in 1894 that the Navy had now "reached a point of perfection to which the whole world yields its unstinted admiration," in 1895 that the Navy "certainly is small, but superior to all others in its discipline." Consequently things could not be so bad. The Emperor was probably exaggerating the matter, as he was apt to do, and alarming people unintentionally. But the nation was not to be scared. *Bange machen gilt nicht*,[1] says the German proverb. In the midst of all this the Kaiser received indirect support from the quarter whence he had least expected it. The Chino-Japanese War ended with the Peace of Shimoniseki on April 17, 1895; but only a week later Germany, Russia, and France, supported by Spain, laid before Japan a whole series of requests which she, much against her will, was obliged to accede to. This action on the part of these three Great Powers, which in Germany's case gave her citizens the right to settle in the Chinese districts of Hankow and Tientsin, awoke strong disapproval in England, and when the Kaiser, in August of the same year, showed himself at Cowes Regatta he felt as though the popular indignation struck against him like a taut sail.

But now, as always, he had the usual phrases at his command: the German Navy's eagerness to learn from its English model, his personal pride at being a British Admiral, the memorable day when he first hoisted his flag on the old *Dreadnought*, etc. But it was no good.

The English Press, with the ultra-Conservative *Standard* at its head, gave him to understand that he would do well to take a lesson in political wisdom from his grandmother, Queen Victoria. It was impossible that he could surpass her in acute-

[1] Scaring is no use.

ness, and as a matter of fact people asked no more than that he should show himself worthy of his descent on his mother's side. As a more cogent argument, it was pointed out that the British Government always wished to be on friendly terms with the German Empire, but that the Kaiser's policy had a leaning towards diplomatic experiments which had a most disquieting effect. Germany ought to remember that England's goodwill was of much greater value to her than any other diplomatic connections. These articles roused displeasure in Germany, where they were interpreted as an attack, not only on the Kaiser's person but also on the Empire, and both the official and semi-official Press were ready with a reply. England openly demanded that " Navyless Germany " should not dare to cross her path as a colonizing Power. But Germany did not intend to be put aside in the pursuit of her legitimate interests. From that moment the importance of a sea-going fleet of powerful ships began to dawn upon the German mind. People saw that there was a natural connection between naval policy and colonial policy. Germany's action towards Japan and the displeasure this circumstance aroused in England gave new support to German naval policy, and this found a direct expression in the Kaiser's famous telegram to President Kruger on the occasion of Dr. Jameson's ill-starred raid into the Transvaal towards the end of 1895 : " I congratulate you most heartily on the fact that in your own strength and without appealing to the help of friendly Powers, you and your people have been successful in securing peace for yourselves against the armed bands which broke into your country, and also in safeguarding your independence against attack from outside." It has been known from the very first that this telegram, which generally goes by the name of "the Kruger telegram," was not due to any "impulsive action" on the part of the Kaiser. *The Times* at once announced that it had been composed in the Chancellor's palace, where Marschall von Bieberstein, then Foreign Secretary, Herr von Hollmann, Minister for Naval Affairs, and others had been summoned to a conference with the Kaiser. Another version, which in reality amounts to the same thing—namely, that a deliberate State action took place—stated that the telegram was composed by the Secretary for Foreign Affairs and submitted to the Kaiser, ready for signature, in the presence of the gentlemen mentioned. The Kaiser was decidedly opposed to burdening the telegraphic cables with this quite superfluous and, from a political point of view, highly doubtful telegram; but the Foreign Secretary, whose diplomatic abilities, as far as we can judge, were considerably overrated by his colleagues, at any rate, after he had succeeded in getting into office,[1] adhered to the view that it was necessary for the German Empire to take action in the affair by means of an Imperial dispatch. Besides, in this the Kaiser could depend on the

---

[1] As an example of the small esteem he enjoyed on first taking office, among other things on account of his complete ignorance of foreign languages, it may be quoted that in the Diplomatic Corps he was known, not as *M. le ministre aux affaires étrangères* (the Minister for Foreign Affairs), but as *M. le ministre étranger aux affaires* (the Minister with no knowledge of affairs).

THE JUBILEE YEAR 117

general approval of the German nation. This last argument proved convincing. The Kaiser not only gave his consent to the telegram, but he also ordered that it should be published in the Press.

The Kruger telegram made a great sensation throughout the world, but especially in England and Germany. There were at first in England a good many people who were willing to excuse the Kaiser, though they thought it rather remarkable that Queen Victoria's grandson—the annual guest at the Cowes Regatta and the constant, demonstrative exponent of his friendly feelings towards England—should be the very first man to express his joy to the Boers on the occasion of a British reverse. But he never could leave the telegraph-wires alone when anything happened, and this was a first-class opportunity of meddling with them.

If things had stopped at this benevolent interpretation on the part of the British public, there is reason to believe that the whole disturbance would have died down very quickly. But it very soon became evident that the whole incident was nothing short of a fixed attempt to collide with British colonial interests in Africa. Among other things, it was ascertained that just as Dr. Jameson was completing his preparations the Germans had exerted strong pressure on the Portuguese Government to allow the passage of German troops through the district of Delagoa Bay. This decided the matter, and what at first had been only a temporary feeling of displeasure now turned into downright national fury, which swept England from end to end and destroyed the last remnants of sympathy with the Kaiser.

He continued to remain on friendly terms with his English relatives, whom he visited privately during the next year. Politically, however, England was closed to him, and it was not until five years later, on a raw, chilly January day in 1901, by the death-bed of Queen Victoria—after he had disappointed the Boers in all their expectations, and their fate was, in fact, already sealed—that a kind of reconciliation was made between the Kaiser and the British people. But time has never allowed the Kruger telegram to sink into oblivion, and even after his—to the Germans—painfully open-hearted disclosures in 1908, to which we shall refer later, there remained in the British people a sense of distrust which rankled continuously up to the outbreak of the Great War.

On the other hand, the Kruger telegram aroused perfectly unanimous enthusiasm in Germany. The people took it as a proof that the German colonial policy had now been led into a definite path, that those in the highest quarters really meant to develop the German-African Colonial Empire which had been founded by Bismarck, but which had been crippled later by the Heligoland Agreement. Feeling in Germany was in favour of the Boers. The Kaiser had interpreted the nation's feelings just as they wished them to be interpreted in the face of an occurrence like the Jameson Raid. It created sympathy for him in Germany, even among those who were not generally reckoned among his admirers, that he had now aroused public wrath against himself in England ; he no longer represented himself only, but the German people as well, who were included in the British displeasure and who quite instinctively felt a satisfaction in returning it. He therefore had the overwhelming bulk of the nation with him when at a State banquet at the Palace in Berlin on January 18, 1896—the twenty-fifth anniversary of the Imperial proclamation in Versailles—he expressed himself in the following remarkable words: " The German Empire has become a World-Empire. Thousands of our countrymen live abroad in the most distant parts of the world. German manufactures, German science, German industry, travel across the ocean. The value of German goods afloat may be estimated at thousands of millions. It is your duty, gentlemen, to see that you help me to incorporate this Greater Germany permanently into the old Fatherland. . . . You will loyally and devotedly assist me to discharge my duty, not only to our countrymen at home but to those thousands of our countrymen who dwell afar, so that when they need my protection I may have the power to extend it to them."

CHAPTER X

A FUTURE ON THE SEAS

THE Kaiser's grandiloquent speech on the "Greater" Germany of the future—the Colonial Empire beyond the sea which was to be welded together into an organic whole with the mother-country—gave *The Times* an opportunity of putting two very practical questions: In what hitherto unappropriated quarter of the globe is this new empire to be carved out, or else how and from whom is it to be conquered? By whom is it to be populated?

These questions, which cannot be called unreasonable from the British point of view, had, however, a certain sting in them which made official Germany smart?

Visionaries! Where will you get to without a Navy?

Here we touch the central point of German colonial policy. It had begun to make conquests beyond the sea, and had inaugurated a *Weltpolitik* without having a fleet which was qualified to support the policy, and with an administration which was entirely devoid of either understanding or interest in the matter. Caprivi, showing a knowledge of men which would have done credit even to his predecessor, had established a Colonial Office with an independent head. Its object was to defeat official ambitions by clearing out the city bureaucrats, who looked upon colonial policy as a tiresome but unavoidable consequence of Germany's being a Great Power.

William II had seen the connection between colonial and naval policy earlier than the majority of his countrymen—more from inborn love of conquest than from a true political instinct. But, unfortunately, he had been quite unable to impress the German people with the same view. He could not do so, even as he could not gain German confidence in other directions, because of his impatience and annoyance at all opposition, his fits of passion, his constant unmasking of his batteries, to use a military term, and above everything else his demonstrative assurances of friendship towards England, which only made matters worse.

He had already referred to the affair of Kiauchau in his speech on Versailles Day, but when speaking at the opening of the Reichstag in November 1897, he used more moderate language than might have been expected. He attended in person, and announced the introduction of the motion subsequently passed in the form of the so-called "First Navy Act."

"The development of our Fleet," he said in his historical speech from the Throne, "does not correspond to what Germany is compelled to ask of her naval forces. The Fleet is inadequate to guarantee the safety of our harbours and coasts against a blockade or other enterprises of the enemy in the event of hostile complications. Nor has it kept pace with the vigorous growth of our interests beyond the sea. While German trade shares to an increasing extent in the commerce of the world, the number of our ships of war is inadequate to afford to our countrymen in foreign countries that degree of protection which is worthy of the position of Germany, and thereby also we fail to offer them that support which only a well-developed Navy is in a position to give. Although we do not attempt to rival naval Powers of the first rank, Germany must be put in a position to maintain her prestige among the nations of the world by arming herself adequately. To this end it is necessary that the Home Fleet should be strengthened, and that the number of ships intended for foreign service in time of peace should be increased."

In order to emphasize still further the importance of his words, he even went so far as to make a personal appeal to the members of the Reichstag, after the reading of the speech, begging them to assist him to keep his Imperial oath " to defend the unity of the Empire abroad."

It required, however, great efforts to force the Bill through the Reichstag, as the members, in spite of a persevering lobby agitation and some point-blank threats on the part of the Kaiser to strike down the opposition, did not feel themselves called upon to make any concessions. In order to leave no means untried, the Kaiser even had recourse to the unusual expedient of addressing an appeal to the nation in the form of a circular, which, on a basis of statistics, informed the general public of the regrettable fact that the German

A FUTURE ON THE SEAS

Navy, notwithstanding the launching of several new ships during the first half of the 'nineties, was proportionately weaker, compared with the Navies of the other Great Powers, than was the case at the Kaiser's accession. This information really implied a sharp criticism on "the new course" as well as on himself for having allowed Caprivi, who did not wish to take up the cudgels in the Reichstag on behalf of the Navy, to cut down the most necessary expenditure. The result was that naval development had really come to a standstill —involving even retrogression. But at this moment it looked as if the majority of the nation was willing to forget even that. Instinctively the pendulum began to swing towards him, with the one exception of the Socialists—the *Vaterlandslose Gesellen*,[1] as he had styled them some months before in a telegram to his brother Prince Henry. From that moment the game was practically won. The rest of the agitation was worked by the Navy League, which was founded in April 1898, some weeks after the First Navy Act had been passed by the Reichstag.

This association, the name of which will always be connected with the reconstruction of the German Navy about the year 1900, had for a number of years carried out its programme with unequalled ability; it was a perfect masterpiece of agitation, whatever view might be held as to the agitation itself.

Together with the Naval Department, under the leadership of Admiral von Tirpitz,[2] the Navy

[1] Unpatriotic fellows.
[2] Dismissed 1916, some months after the appearance of this book in the Norwegian original.

League, under Admiral von Koester, has worked more quietly and more steadily than any other administrative machine in the whole Empire. Herr von Tirpitz introduced the naval Bills into the Reichstag, and bore the burden and heat of the day in order to push them through. Herr von Koester undertook the manipulation of the people at large, overcame the element of inertia always present in them, and made the pendulum of thought swing in the desired direction. Undoubtedly the Kaiser, as we have mentioned before, tried, through his naval Cabinet, to exert an undue influence in the management of affairs, and several of those types of ships which he had introduced as first-class [1] had to be abandoned later as complete failures. The essential thing, however, was that Herr von Tirpitz and Herr von Koester were allowed to remain at their posts, undisturbed by all those Imperial squalls which in the course of years had blown so many other capable men away from their positions.

The result was that by degrees there grew up a Germany with a naval and colonial programme far more strongly defined than it had been in the speech from the Throne of 1897, and, above all, backed by a national will which carried considerably farther than the Imperial words. To the Kaiser the Navy,to a certain extent, has always been a theme for declamation. For the nation it has embodied a reality, which has entered into its life and influenced its development. Accordingly,

---

[1] As, for example, the so-called *Hertha* class (cruisers) which had to be taken out of active service long ago, and pass into the category of training ships.

A FUTURE ON THE SEAS

the nation was very slow to respond to the appeal, but when it did respond it was prepared to take all the consequences. It is necessary to grasp this fact in order to understand the agitation which so deeply influenced the German mind and outlook during the fourteen years from the beginning of the new century up to the Great War. It was as though the nation were seized by a sense of the need for expansion—a kind of *sehnsuchtvolles Hungerleiden nach dem Unerreichlichen*,[1] as it was put by a representative of the Reichstag nearly ten years ago in a happy quotation from Goethe. The work of the Navy League in this direction has exercised such an important influence that it becomes the salient feature of this period of the reign of William II.

The Navy League at the outbreak of the Great War included more than three hundred local associations, with a total membership of nearly four millions. Through its monthly paper, *Die Flotte*, which had a circulation of over 350,000 copies, through countless pamphlets and lectures, the League for a number of years has succeeded in arousing an exceptional interest in the Fleet. With praiseworthy understanding of the old saying that "they that are whole need not a physician, but they that are sick," the League had concentrated its efforts on the interior of the country—wherever there might be an abode of doubt and ignorance. In the Bavarian highlands, far in East Prussia, and in the Rhine province, where people formerly lived in a condition of primitive ignorance with regard to maritime affairs, the practised

[1] A yearning hunger after the unattainable.

lecturers of the League were at work. A score of cinematographs, owned by the League, made known the greatness and growth of the Fleet, the marvels of mechanism, and the wonderful discoveries and improvements. The leading men were passed by in review, the Kaiser at their head, of course, as the creator of the whole. Every single year thousands of school children and their teachers from the interior of the country were conveyed, on the initiative of the League, to the coast, to the military and naval ports and docks, in order that they might see all the ships which the Kaiser was building for the defence of Germany. The Imperial catchwords were repeated till every school child knew them and no average citizen could doubt their accuracy. "Our future which lies on the seas," "Neptune's trident, which must rest in the hand of Germany," "the free ocean, which is an indispensable condition of Germany's greatness," "the bitter need for a Navy," etc.—all these phrases gradually sank into the consciousness of the people, though they were not roused until they observed, or fancied they observed, opposition to their legitimate claims.

These feelings of anger, however, were not sufficient in themselves; they needed to be artificially stimulated. In this respect the Navy League has been unceasingly at work—particularly whenever it has been necessary to support the experimental foreign policy of the Kaiser. "The Fatherland in Danger," "Perfidious Albion," "The British Peril," "England the Enemy," "The Next War," etc.—all these are the titles of pamphlets dating from the years immediately preceding the war.

They show the nature of the agitation and the way in which it was carried on—with the fixed purpose of creating a constantly growing Fleet. The programme was, to put it briefly, to secure "Neptune's trident" at whatever cost. It was an aspiration, like the America Cup and the Atlantic record.

In the whole of this agitation the Kaiser was, if not exactly the central figure, at any rate the official symbol. His telegrams and speeches concerning the Navy and *Weltpolitik* increased in number after the passing of the First Navy Act and the establishment of the Navy League. He congratulated the German confederate princes, complimented the managers of the League on various occasions, gave orders to a detachment of torpedo-boats to steam up the Rhine and touch at Cologne "in order to bring a greeting from the sea." They went farther and farther inland, in spite of all obstacles, passed through Hessen and Baden, and only stopped at Strassburg. Even Bavaria, with its highland associations, was visited, and one day in 1900 the flotilla steered into Germersheim, where the little Queich River, after a short course eastward, runs into the Rhine.

The princes of the German Confederation expressed, both personally and on behalf of their subjects, their loyal feelings towards the Kaiser on the occasion of these unusual visits. The Kaiser telegraphed expressing his thanks in return. He was "convinced that national enthusiasm, comprehension, and interest with regard to our task on the sea is surely increasing in the

German people," and that his "exertions to secure a strong Navy for Germany" would be crowned with success.

He watched his ships being launched—in Kiel, in Hamburg, Wilhelmshaven—*Kaiser Wilhelm der Grosse* and *Kaiser Karl der Grosse* within a few months of each other in 1899, and *Wittelsbach* in 1900. They were the first practical results of the Navy Act and of the labours of the Navy League. Each of these ships was "a new piece of the floating bulwarks of the Fatherland"—a proof that Germany had at length awakened to the understanding of "how forcibly the waves of the ocean beat upon the gates of our nation and compel us, as a great people, to assert our place in the world"—in other words, to embark on a *Weltpolitik*. "The freedom of the sea is indispensable to the greatness of Germany. But the ocean reminds us also that on it and beyond it no great decision may henceforward be made without Germany and the German Emperor. I am not one of those who think that our German nation, under the leadership of its princes, conquered and bled thirty years ago, in order to let itself be put aside now when great events are being decided abroad. If we submitted to that, it would be all over with the position of Germany in the world, and I do not intend to let that come to pass. To use the most suitable and, if need be, the most drastic means, regardless of consequences, towards the attainment of our end—such is my duty and my greatest privilege."

The complete change which had taken place in

the nation could not have been emphasized more clearly than it was, by word and deed, by writings and by pictures. Yet we must not forget that from the very beginning of the new century there were many who resisted—temperate newspapers and magazines and neutral business corporations —as, for instance, the Chamber of Commerce at Bremen as early as 1901 in its Annual Report. The tendency towards exaggeration, now that the Kaiser himself was involved in the movement, was certain to arouse anxiety in all who were able to see beyond the actual moment. " The German nation becomes more and more defiant in its language when discussing official matters," wrote the well-known journal *Die Grenzboten* in January 1902. " It is lamentable to notice how the tone on such matters has changed during the last ten years—it is high time to stop pouring oil upon the fire." As we have already indicated, these and similar wise words did not receive the attention they deserved, especially on account of the disastrous theory of the European " ring policy " towards Germany, which already had begun to obtain power over the minds of men. The Imperial speech just quoted is particularly illuminating on this point—and it was not to be the last.

Here was the German nation on the threshold of the twentieth century, which the Kaiser, in spite of the almanack and the rest of the world, had decreed should begin on January 1, 1900.

" The German nation is like a gallant race-horse," said the Kaiser in a speech given at Stettin.

"He will not allow any other to get ahead of him, but will keep the lead."

And so the German nation took a spurt forward in the grey dawn of the twentieth century, while its competitors had still 365 days left out of the nineteenth.

CHAPTER XI

THE END OF THE FIRST TEN YEARS

THE significant change in the national views of Germany outlined in the preceding chapter practically coincided with Prince Hohenlohe's Chancellorship. It was the period of Imperial autocracy *par excellence*—the high summer of might, when ambition spread its wings and shaped its course towards a distant goal. It was inaugurated in a reactionary fashion by an appeal on the part of the Kaiser to the Prussian nobility to support him in the struggle for religion, morality, and order against the revolutionary party ; but it was obvious that no moment could have been less suitable for the launching of such a policy. The so-called " Revolt Act," which was introduced into the Reichstag shortly after Caprivi's fall, will stand out for all time as a remarkable proof of political short-sightedness in William II and his advisers.

The discussion on the Bill, which extended through nearly the whole of the session of 1895, contributed largely to embitter the jubilee year, and created that widespread discontent and indifference which we have already mentioned. The Bill was ingenuous to the last degree because religion and national ambitions, Christian socialism, and greedy desires for conquest across the seas cannot easily be cultivated side by side. Here Caprivi showed a true instinct and a sound, Conservative, and thoroughly honourable view which was based on something of a historical tradition. A generation earlier Roon, the famous War Minister of William I, had been anxious lest Prussia's position as the leading power in Germany should have a demoralizing effect on the strongly monarchical and ecclesiastical character of the great majority of the Prussian people, and therefore he held out for a long time against the Bismarckian policy. Caprivi was troubled lest the ambitiously conceived colonial policy which William II had taken up should transform the old-fashioned honourable type of contented and loyal Germans into a vulgar, pushing race, with British individualism and American haste. This fear was undoubtedly justified from the psychological point of view. But even if Caprivi had been allowed to continue in office as Chancellor, the German community, when he entered public life, was already so deeply affected by social contradictions and by all the questions connected with them, and so distinctly materialistic in all its commercial morality and its views on economic questions that the thing could no longer be stayed.

Prince Hohenlohe, who had less character than Caprivi, and who, above all, was not troubled by the latter's moral anxieties, was distinctly better able to adopt such a policy. His great age was also an excuse for him, as it cannot well be expected that any strong resistance to Imperial desires can be offered by a man of seventy-six who earlier in life had not shown much independence. With Hohenlohe official irresponsibility appeared in public life in a way which people had never before seen or imagined possible. He was born in 1819, and for many years he had pursued a successful career in accordance with the theory which he had once jokingly recommended, that " a young man who wants to make his way in the world ought to have a good black coat and keep his mouth shut." He had been Ambassador in Paris and latterly Governor of Alsace-Lorraine—a post to which he had retired after he had been Prussian Minister of State in 1884. At that time he had tendered his resignation, after having been six months in office, on the grounds that the official duties attached to the position were beyond his powers and his strength. Now—ten years later—he allowed himself to be appointed, not only Prussian Minister of State but Imperial Chancellor. He tells us that he at first declined the office, and only after two days' pressure gave way to the Imperial request ; but unfortunately the statement is not quite correct, when the editor of his famous " Memoirs " (which in many respects are such an excellent source of information concerning the age of William II) makes the observation that a " sense of imperative patriotic duty seems to have decided the Prince to follow the Imperial call in spite of his serious misgivings." The fact is that Prince Hohenlohe was finally given his choice between the Chancellorship and dismissal from State service altogether. He chose the first alternative because his active nature could not reconcile itself to the thought of complete idleness even in advanced years. But it goes without saying that he was too clever to nurse any illusions as to the permanence of his new appointment.

"The difficulty of my new position lies in His Majesty's unexpected decisions," he notes in his Diary for January 14, 1895. But the jubilee year, with all its political perplexities, not least so in the shape of ministerial crises and intrigues behind the scenes, taught him to act with a dexterity hardly to be expected in a man of his age. A year later, on January 26, 1896, he writes to one of his friends :—

"I should have answered you earlier, but alternations of jubilee festivities and crises claim the whole of my time. As a rule the crises pass off quite peaceably after having kept my friends in suspense for some days. For the moment His Majesty agrees with me and will have no other Chancellor but me. Under the circumstances, therefore, I am, in spite of all my shortcomings, the best Chancellor he could have."

"And what would be gained by a change in the Chancellorship?" he asks in another place in his Diary, after having mentioned the existence of a strong opposition in the Reichstag bent on "bringing me into discredit with His Majesty. Naturally nothing but conflicts with the Reichstag. But conflicts with the Reichstag will lead to dissolution and new elections. Dissolution, again, leads to *coups d'état*, and *coups d'état* to conflicts with the Confederate Princes, to civil war, to the dissolution of the German Empire. Then foreign countries would not keep quiet, but would interfere—at least, France would."

The observation is brilliantly clear in its argument from cause to effect. In the face of such far-reaching possibilities it was natural that the Kaiser and his Chancellor should agree, both in their own interest and in the interests of the Fatherland. It appeared, in fact, as if the Kaiser were increasingly satisfied with his elderly Chancellor, and on several occasions he took the opportunity of congratulating him on the political success he had obtained.

In 1897 there came an opportunity to celebrate a new jubilee. A hundred years had passed since William I was born, and because of the eminent part he had taken in the reconstruction of the Fatherland, and because of his high moral qualities, it was right both from the historical and human points of view that his memory should receive the honour due to it.

For William II, who long ago had lost all sense of proportion where his grandfather was concerned, this event became a new and elaborate subject for declamation, with all the phrases of 1895, and even earlier. The old Kaiser, whose strong points were his modesty, his moral dignity, and, with regard to his greatest achievement—his unqualified admission that his own work ranked second—was made to rise again on his hundredth anniversary as the creator of the whole. He was now the man with "the great thoughts always lying ready in his brain," and waiting to be released at the psychological moment. "Under God's guidance there were by his side many wise and capable advisers, who had the honour of carrying out his thoughts. But they were simply tools for his exalted will, and vessels filled with that exalted Emperor's spirit." With this mistaken piety towards his grandfather's memory, the Kaiser was not satisfied with disturbing the very foundations of fact and establishing hopeless confusion between cause and effect. He felt that he must dramatize him in the literal sense of the word. Together with the author Ernst von Wildenbruch —a novelist who was on a par with the Kaiser's French ideal Georges Ohnet and not much better as a dramatist—he wrote a festival play entitled "Willehalm." He was present at the rehearsals, thoroughly amused himself with the actors and actresses who were taking parts, and gave advice and directions with the confidence of an old stage hand.

He was particularly eager in instructing an actress to whom had been assigned the difficult task of representing "the German soul."

"You must not smile in this part," he said. "The German soul is profoundly serious—and always the same," he added. "You must express it in the whole of your bearing—yes, even in your drapery. It must flow from head to foot in one unbroken line."

But the German soul was not only forbidden to smile; it was not even permitted to criticize. That "spirit of disobedience" to which the Kaiser had so often referred was a thing with which he would have no dealings. During the students' torchlight procession to the palace on the occasion of the hundred years' jubilee he received a deputation from the procession, and adjured them to make it their endeavour that the German people should give up that carping and grumbling which was, unhappily, far too frequent among them.

The speech made a sensation, and with good cause. There was no visible occasion for it ; quite the contrary. The Kaiser had come direct from a banquet with the German princes, and wherever he looked about him from the palace balcony, loyalty beamed towards him in the illuminations and torches. Yet the thought of the discontented elements in the Empire was the strongest one within him. In a speech five years before he had recommended those who were dissatisfied " to shake off the German dust from your shoes and seek out a new home for yourselves under a brighter sky." Now he was not particularly disposed to repeat this sentence, because he knew that the army of malcontents had considerably increased during the last few years, and that it would not be advisable for people to take him too literally. He only wished to hammer it into the youthful students on an evening which they were likely to remember that it must be their task to promote within the Empire a correct way of thinking, and to make loyal citizens who were satisfied with the existing state of things, and who were unwilling to express any criticism whatsoever.

The nation was to place " the great Emperor," whose centenary was now being celebrated, " on the throne " of its admiration and love, " to gather in crowds round his memory, as the Spaniards did of yore round the old Cid." In truth, he had done great things for the nation and had set it a shining example. But especially had he "raised for us princes an altar which it is our duty to keep holy—the altar of monarchy by Divine Right—monarchy with its heavy duties, its incessant, abiding labour and pains, its awful responsibility to the Creator alone—a responsibility from which no human being, no minister, no representative assembly, no nation, is able to deliver the Prince."

With such a view of his position, it was only natural that he had nothing to say to the nation on the tenth anniversary of his accession to the throne. As an alternative he gathered his regiments of bodyguards together at Potsdam on June 16, 1898, and addressed them in a long speech: "The greatest inheritance which my illustrious grandfather and father bequeathed to me, and which I entered upon with joy and pride, is the Army. To the Army I addressed my first speech when I ascended the throne; to the Army I direct my words once more, now at the beginning of a new decade. It was with deep anxiety that I took up the crown. On all sides men doubted me, on all sides I encountered misunderstandings. Only one had confidence in me, only one believed in me—and this was the Army." In this cry of distress there was in fact an admission—that to-day, after ten years, he had not advanced much. The reason for this was evident to every one except himself. Like Joseph of Austria, a little more than a century before, he was under the unfortunate delusion that "good intentions are sufficient to secure a prosperous reign." No more fatal mistake can be made by a ruler than that; no theory is more likely to delude him and to encourage the fancy that he is something of a misinterpreted genius. The whole of William II's reign during the 'nineties rests upon this view. Therefore in reality he estranged himself more and more from his people, in spite of his never-ending speeches and journeys, his parades and receptions of princes, his exaggerated advertising of the name of Germany all over the habitable globe. All this, however, was not what the nation primarily desired. It wanted, above everything else, to be left alone—a feeling connected with its feeble interest in public life and its indifference towards the parliamentary form of government. This element of inertia, which always creates a favourable soil for personal rule, naturally did not enter for a moment into the Imperial calculations. He governed as he spoke, without regard to the conditions around him, solely occupied with whatever was astir in his restless world of thought. The system he represented, which from its very nature ought to be a model of stability, was so full of surprises that the nation could not feel at ease for a single day. Every morning people ran the risk of waking up to find something new had happened. Ministers changed with almost uncanny rapidity. During the first eight years of his reign the Kaiser saw nineteen new Ministers around him, and by 1898 " people had ceased to count them," said a German writer. Later on they were changed at a rate which yields nothing in comparison with the most unstable conditions under a vacillating parliamentary system.

Some of these Ministers were removed amid the most poignant regrets on the part of the nation, among them—in 1896—the distinguished Minister of War, Bronsart, who had an exceptional reputation in the Army. Others disappeared in silence, the victims of intrigues and hidden machinations. All this was accompanied by a passion for investigation and reform in all directions, for new ideas and experiments, the moment that the Kaiser's active brain thought it had hit upon something fresh in one direction or another. Army organization, social policy, commercial and even naval policy, were altered by fits and starts.

A few weeks before the Reichstag met to discuss the First Navy Bill, an event took place which was to be of deep significance in the development of Germany's colonial and naval policy.

During the first days of November 1897 a telegram was received stating that certain Roman Catholic missionaries of German descent had been murdered in the southern part of the Chinese province of Shantung. Ten days later a German squadron had already entered the bay of Kiau-Chau and annexed the district in the name of the Kaiser. It was no new plan which was thus put into execution. Germany had long wished to obtain a firm footing in Northern China, and Herr von Tirpitz, during his stay in Eastern Asia in 1896, as Admiral of the German squadron, had fixed his attention on Kiau-Chau, the central situation of which and its excellent hinterland plainly made it an ideal spot for colonization. Unfortunately, no German missionaries had then been killed, so that Herr von Tirpitz was obliged to turn back from the Promised Land like a new

Moses, having only beheld it from afar. But now that an opportunity presented itself the way became quite clear. By the diplomatic proceedings instituted between the German and the Chinese Governments immediately after the German landing at Kiau-Chau, China was compelled to punish the murderers and to depose the Governor of Shantung as being the "moral instigator" of the murder—a philosophical definition which never has been quite clear to the followers of Confucius. In addition, the Chinese Government had to pay an indemnity of 20,000 taels to the Roman Catholic Mission and to build three "penance" churches and seven Mission buildings, making a total value of 200,000 taels. The best part of the whole affair, however, was the treaty concerning Kiau-Chau, by which Germany "leased" this valuable district for ninety-nine years.

But it was not enough to carry on diplomatic negotiations only. Germany's first conquest in Eastern Asia naturally had to be inaugurated in a way which the nation and the whole world would observe. With this object, the Kaiser sent his brother, Prince Henry, out to China in command of a squadron in December 1897. At a farewell dinner in Berlin he addressed him in a speech to the effect that the expedition which was now about to start was "the logical sequence of what my grandfather of blessed memory and his great Chancellor established in the world of politics, and what our admirable father gained on the field of battle—the first practical recognition on the part of the recently united and reconstructed

Empire of its responsibilities beyond the sea." He therefore adjured his brother to uphold Germany's interests in such a way "that it may be clear to every European out there, to every German out there, and, above all, to every foreigner on whose soil we may be and with whom we may have to deal, that the German Michael has planted his shield, blazoned with the Imperial eagle, firmly in that soil, ready to extend to each and all the protection they may require. But should any one attempt to affront us or to infringe our lawful rights, then do you strike out with your mailed fist and wreathe round your young brow the laurels which no one in the whole German Empire will begrudge you."

The Prince was deeply impressed, and promised to set out "and proclaim the gospel of your Majesty's exalted person."

Not only in the Far East of Asia, but also in the West, it was needful to strike a blow for German interests and for the "Imperial gospel."

This work the Kaiser took upon his own shoulders in October 1898.

He had—to use his own words—from his very earliest youth felt "a burning desire to visit the holy places where our Lord and Saviour walked on earth and accomplished the work of redemption." Now an opportunity offered itself for the fulfilment of this desire. On a site which had been presented to his father—then Crown Prince Frederick William of Prussia—during a visit to Palestine, a Protestant church had been built, in order that God's Word should be preached in it according to the Protestant creed in the German language, and that the name of Jesus Christ should be praised in the German tongue.

But—as an official German jubilee publication expressed it—however much the Kaiser's journey to Jerusalem had been inspired by purely religious motives, there was also a highly political significance attaching to it. In simpler words, this is equivalent to saying that the main object of the expedition was to promote commercial intercourse between Germany and the Orient through Turkey by establishing a more definite programme for the Bagdad railway. It is this policy—one of the most deliberate results of German initiative and the investment of German capital in the last generation—which is now on its trial in the Balkan Peninsula and in Asia Minor.

From an ethical point of view, the moment was not exactly a happy one for a crusade under the gracious protection of the Sultan. Abdul Hamid still stood branded by public opinion in Europe and America after the slaughter of his Armenian subjects in 1896, and Gladstone's terrible name for him—" the Murderer on the Throne "—had gained new reality a few months before through the death of the great statesman. But those friendly relations between Abdul Hamid and William II which had been first established in 1889 had lost nothing of their warmth during the nine years that had passed. The visit to Constantinople on the way out to Palestine resolved itself into something like a triumph, and the needful concessions for the Bagdad railway were granted under the most liberal conditions.

In Jerusalem the Kaiser dedicated the new

"Church of the Redeemer"—as it was called—
in a lengthy speech.

"From Jerusalem," said he, "came the Light of
the world, in whose lustre our German nation has
become great and glorious. . . . Just as nearly two
thousand years ago, so also to-day shall there ring
out from this spot to all the world the words which
embody our dearest hopes, 'Peace on earth!' As
on this solemn day I renew the vow of my ancestors
now at rest in God: 'As for me and my house,
we will serve the Lord,' so do I call upon you to
make the same vow. May the noblest ornaments
of the German nation always continue to be fear
of God, charity, patience in suffering, and diligence
in work."

Yet it was not these words which attracted the
attention of the world.

The main interest gathered round his speech in
Damascus on the way back from Palestine, when,
with a reference to the memory of the great Sultan
Saladin—"one of the most knightly monarchs of
any period"—he expressed his thanks to Abdul
Hamid in the following words:—

"Let the Sultan and the three hundred millions
of Mohammedans throughout the world who
honour him as their spiritual chief rest assured
that at all times the German Emperor will be
their friend."

CHAPTER XII

THEORY AND FACT

SOME months before the Imperial speech at Damascus, which was such a typical expression of the range of the German world policy, death had severed the last bond which linked the new period with Germany's heroic age. Bismarck had died on July 30, 1898, an event which had been anticipated for months, but which, however, made an overwhelming impression when the inexorable fact was realized.

There was amongst those whose verdict had any value whatever only one opinion—that the strife which had led to his disappearance from public life eight years before had coincided with a continued decline in the power and influence of Germany. In spite of journeys and speeches in north and south, and official embraces of various European rulers on half a score of railway stations and quays, in spite of letters of congratulations and telegrams of condolence, all testifying to a mental ubiquity far beyond the ordinary, it was obvious to all that German foreign policy throughout the 'nineties was characterized by a lamentable want of skill and management. " The political direction changes continually in the most capricious and aimless manner," said a German writer. " Now it takes immense pains in order to gain the friendship of Russia ; now it pays court to England or France ; and the moment after it comes to loggerheads, now with one Power, now with another, without cause and without conceivable object. It has come to this, that European politics are made in Petersburg, London, Paris, and Vienna, but not in Berlin. . . . We have lost the last remnants of our initiative."

A few examples illustrating these words, which were written in 1897, are not without interest.

The Franco-Russo-German action with regard to Japan, in 1895, had opened the way for better relations between Germany and France, and at one time it even looked as if the two Powers would work together against British interests in North Africa. At the same time Germany had cast her eyes upon the Portuguese colonies in South Africa, with the object of thwarting a possible British attack on the Boer republics, in which event she could calculate on the assistance of France.

During these years the Kaiser was amiability itself towards France, both privately and officially ; but when the Méline Ministry, in the summer of 1898, had to resign on the question of the revision of the Dreyfus case, and a Radical Government stepped in, with Delcassé as Secretary of State for Foreign Affairs, he hastened to put the helm over. It was idle now to think of a reconciliation with France, and almost as impossible to hope for an understanding with England, because, among other things, of the still unsettled question of the Samoa

Islands, which had been pending ever since 1889. In the autumn of 1898 France had to make her well-known withdrawal in the so-called Fashoda incident, about the same time that Lord Kitchener completed his conquest of Sudan in the battle of Omdurman. This was a simply overwhelming defeat for the German policy of expansion in North Africa. But in a speech made before the Waterloo Column in Hanover, the Kaiser still felt obliged to remind his audience of the British and German fraternity of arms, and, as an act of homage to the British Army on the occasion of the Omdurman victory, he called for a cheer for his octogenarian grandmother Queen Victoria, Colonel-in-Chief of the 1st Regiment of Prussian Guards.

The following year the outbreak of the Boer War disclosed the weakness of the German foreign policy in the most convincing manner. By its sudden change of course with regard to France it had closed the way to an eventual Franco-Russo-German alliance, directed against England, whilst by the challenge in the Kruger telegram it had slammed the door against British confidence with a bang which still re-echoed. At the same time the Kaiser by his fiery words to the German nation about "a future on the sea," "Germany, which has become a world-empire," "the great decisions which must no longer be made without Germany and the German Kaiser," "the mailed fist," "the crying need for a Navy," etc., in short by all these words which had no real power behind them, had created a feeling within the German nation which was bound to make the Boer War a simple martyrdom to it. The Kaiser

alone looked at the whole thing in a different light.
He closed his door against old Kruger and
decorated Lord Roberts with the Black Eagle.

But it was not only with respect to foreign
policy that a variable course was steered. In
home affairs there were several unfortunate examples,
of which the most important are those
associated with social policy. We have quoted
Bismarck's remark, that "my young master wishes
to make every one happy," a beautiful sentiment
in youth, and it was beyond doubt this feeling
which from the first suggested to him the idea
of a policy of reconciliation towards the Social
Democrats. But the mighty social development
in Germany during the last generation, and the
circumstances which had led to the industrial
awakening about the middle of the century, had
created an entirely new element in the nation,
a social class with different conceptions of life
and different ideals from those which dominated
official Germany. The whole of this new world
was, and remained, a puzzle to him, which he had
neither time, patience, or ability to understand.
He advanced royally and directly to claim the
national confidence in the ingenuous belief that the
solution of social problems was "as easy as kissing."
At the first opposition he lost patience
and turned round, full of bitterness and angry
words about the ingratitude of the nation. In
1889 he described every Socialist as an enemy of
the Fatherland. In 1890 he wished to start a
policy of reconciliation towards the working class,
and assured them that he would never tire of his
labours in advancing their material welfare,

whether he received "thanks or ingratitude" as his reward. In 1894 his attitude in principle was the same, but the Labour Party had in the past years shown such a decided disinclination to be led in the monarch's patriarchal leading-strings, and displayed so much independent strength and so much confidence in their own future, that the Kaiser could see no alternative but to suggest " an extension of the penal clauses then in force for the protection of law and order." The same year in Königsberg he called upon his subjects to fight for religion, morality, and order against the party of revolt, and on the anniversary of Sedan—as we have heard—he branded the Socialists yet again. But the " Revolt Act " came to nothing, or, more truly, it was re-embodied in " the so-called Prison Act." Speaking at Bielefeld in Westphalia, he hinted at severe punishment for any one who should dare to hinder others in carrying out their work, and in Oeynhausen — also in Westphalia — he announced, the following year, that the alterations in the law were now nearly completed, and they would be laid before the Reichstag during the current year. According to this proposal every German—without respect of persons—who tried to hinder a willing worker in work, or even recommended him to strike, " would be punished with imprisonment." But even as late as 1899 this Bill was still incomplete. In 1900 the Kaiser suddenly turned round, and with an incomprehensible disregard of the fact that the Social Democratic vote in the Reichstag election had risen from 1,400,000 in 1890 to 2,108,000 in 1898, while at the same time the number of their representatives had increased from 35 to 56, he declared that Social Democracy is only a "passing phenomenon ; it will burn itself out." But in the following year he thundered against it afresh—especially in Essen and Breslau—with unusual strength of feeling, and a no less pronounced bitterness and violence in word. "Base and vile deeds" ; "unprincipled agitators who exploit and terrorize the masses" ; "impudent lies"; "attacks upon the altar and the Throne" are some of the expressions which abound in these speeches, which are among the most violent he has made. It is only fair to state that during the 'nineties the Conservative as well as the National Liberal Party constantly recommended him to make an end of the Social Democrats by a *coup d'état*, and that a man of such high standing as Professor Delbrück gave this idea his most unqualified approval as late as 1895, in an article in the *Preussische Jahrbücher*. "It is necessary," he writes, "that a feeling should be aroused among all classes of the population that Social Democracy is a poisonous influence, which can only be checked by the strongest and most united resistance," and it is an established fact that millions of people in Germany thought and felt as did this authority. It is therefore psychologically and politically comprehensible that this advice stimulated the Kaiser, developed his plans, and gave force to his expressions. But it is equally undeniable that old Professor Mommsen—the gifted historian of Rome—was right when he protested against this conception in the unprejudiced words : "An end must be made of the superstition, which is just as false as it is foolish, that the nation is divided into a law-abiding party on one side and a revolutionary party on the other, and that it is the greatest duty of the citizens of the first-mentioned category to shun the Labour Party as if it were in quarantine for the plague, and to attack it as if it were an enemy of the State."

But it was not only the home and foreign policy which showed signs of instability. Even the management of the Army, the branch of administration where one would least have expected it, swayed in the Imperial gusts of reform. The Kaiser entered upon his reign with the declaration which we have already quoted, that he regarded himself as one with the Army, and for years he was never tired of emphasizing the fact that he looked upon the Army as the *rocher de bronze* on which the Empire rested. The important Acts carried during his reign—one concerning a "two-years' service," the other a reform of the military penal law—show that he had grasped the importance of making the Army popular in the best sense of the word. His noted rescript of 1890 points in the same direction. In this rescript he took up arms against the number of exaggerated social demands to which the officers of the Army were subjected, and which practically barred the way to important and responsible military positions for any but rich men. He emphasized that it was more necessary than ever before to develop strength of character among officers, and to teach them to practise proper self-denial. This could only be done by restricting all the luxury which had crept into the Army—the costly gifts, the too frequent garrison banquets, the exaggeration of private hospitality, etc.—to put it shortly, all that extravagance which only led to the creation of a class of officers involved in debt, with a diminished interest in their profession and lessened power of work. "The moneylender tightens his grip upon the uniformed victims, pursues them through despairing nights and days until they can see no alternative but the revolver, having tried the roulette-board in vain."

The Kaiser noticed all this, and repeatedly expressed his disapproval of games of chance, which had so often given rise to sensational scandals among officers. But he did not hit upon a single positive means of bringing about a change in conditions, by removing any of the outward or inward causes of this lamentable state of things. On the contrary, by a strange lack of reasoning power, he contributed to their increase. By constantly hammering into the public mind that officers and the Army were something of a State within the State, enjoying greater honours and rights and social privileges than the ordinary citizen, he encouraged those very class divisions which he wished to counteract, and led his officers into a wrong conception of their social importance, which received the strongest condemnation even from the officers themselves. It should be observed that the Imperial rescript of 1890 has never been more than words. As late as in 1903, thirteen years after it was issued amidst general sympathy from the whole nation, a German officer of high rank expressed the opinion that the German Army was "on the way to Capua," and in Beyerlein's novel, "Jena or Sedan?" social and economic conditions inside the German Army about the beginning of the new century are exposed with a minuteness which will always constitute a severe charge against "the Supreme War-Lord."

With his passion for everything concerning drill, parades, and manœuvres, and his almost abnormal memory for all sorts of military anniversaries, he kept his Army at work, in a way which has no parallel in any country. It was good in one respect, but it inevitably interfered with working hours—and not least, it created increasing expenses for the officers, who were obliged to take part in endless breakfasts and dinners in honour of the Kaiser and the commemoration of battles and great slaughters, for which he searched the records through the centuries, in every part of his great Empire.

The constant changes in uniform and equipment were a source of a smaller grievance to the officers. There were not only alterations in materials and garments, but also in less important things—braids and cords, aiguillettes and tassels. During the years 1894-6 the scarf on the First Prussian Guards was introduced, condemned, introduced again, and then abolished for good. "The history of that scarf," says a German writer, "can be regarded as symbolic of the nervous anxiety of our time to reach speedy results without any fair inquiry as to how much will be gained by them." Seven years later a senior officer, writing in one of the best Conservative organs in Prussia, calculated that during the years 1888-1903, or, in other words, during the sixteen years in which William II had been the "Supreme War-Lord," thirty important changes of uniform as well as innumerable smaller ones had been made, and that at the most five of them could be described as necessary from the military point of view.

With respect to the advantages of the innumerable Imperial manœuvres which have occupied such a large place in the history of the German Army during the last generation—the record in 1903 was five in the course of one week, all of which were described as complete—opinions also differed in competent circles. Authorities on whose judgment the greatest reliance is felt in Germany have characterized them as "competitive performances resembling sports"; and as to the "imposing cavalry charges" which were among the most effective items in these manœuvres, it has been prophesied long ago that the German nation, in case of war, would have to pay terribly dearly for them. It will be the work of future historians of the present war to decide how far and to what extent this prophecy has been fulfilled. We only mention it as proof that the dramatic element which the Kaiser, in accordance with his nature, has tried to introduce into the very training of the Army has been far from obtaining unanimous approval.

A still more doubtful advantage of these manœuvres was that they were brought into the service of the Imperial cult at the cost of the Fatherland. It was a matter which had awakened concern among many of the best friends of the defence. They were not able to see the logical connection between sham-fights, children excused from school, and the whole wearisome parade of white-clad maidens, garlands, triumphal arches, and magnates bowing to the ground.

For the Kaiser himself it had always been of the very greatest importance to impress the masses, to show them the dazzling spectacle of an Army whose technical training was beyond all praise, and strengthen them in the belief of that Army's invincibility. In dealing with the Army itself he set himself the double task of instilling the value of tradition and the fear of God. To his land forces he addressed the same patriarchal type of language as he did towards his sailors—words full of a "romantic mysticism which stands in a strange and inexplicable contrast to those modern views of which the Kaiser is also an exponent," to quote a German author. An expression which is frequently on his lips is that the Christian faith and the military qualities are organically connected. "He who is not a good Christian is not a good man, nor is he a Prussian soldier, and under no circumstances can he perform what is required of a soldier in the Prussian Army."

Japan's victory over Russia in 1904-5 gave a severe shock to the Imperial theory on the superiority of Christian soldiers. He perceived the need of an explanation. "We must not conclude from the Japanese victory," he said, "the victory of a pagan people over a Christian people, that Buddha is superior to Christ. When Russia was beaten in the war with Japan, her defeat was mainly due to the fact that Christianity in Russia is at a sadly low level, while the Japanese possess many Christian virtues." It caused him anxiety, however, lest Christianity in the German nation was also in a bad way, and he doubted whether " we Germans, in case of war, would be justified in praying to God for victory."

CHAPTER XIII

THE TRIUMPH OF CÆSARISM

AGAINST this background of political and military variableness there stands out with dramatic effect the expedition which was sent out to China during the summer and autumn of 1900 to join in the suppression of the so-called " Boxer riots." These " riots," which have been so admirably described by Mr. Putnam West in his " Indiscreet Letters from Peking," were, in fact, a justifiable outburst of indignation and shame on the part of official China at all the humiliations to which the Empire for years past had been subjected by foreign countries. Through a wisely managed agitation, the wires of which were gathered together in the hand of the crafty and energetic Dowager Empress Tsu-Hsi, who with considerable justice has been called " China's Catherine II," the " Boxer riots " had already begun to make headway in 1899. In January 1900 the Ambassadors of the Powers in Peking began to notice the movement, whose strongly marked anti-reform and anti-foreign character was more and more noticeable every day. Two secret societies, with the unpleasant names of " The Red Fist " and " The Great Knife," felt themselves, for some reason or other, particularly embittered at the German annexation of Kiau-Chau, and also behaved in such a threatening manner that the Powers' Ambassadors demanded that the two societies should be suppressed as "dangerous to the State and unfriendly to foreigners," and that their members should be punished. The demand occasioned prolonged but naturally quite fruitless negotiations with the Chinese Government, while at the same time the movement grew at a furious pace. In the early part of the summer the Dowager Empress and her advisers let the mask fall, and the position now became so critical that the Powers, out of regard for their Ambassadors' personal safety, found it necessary to send out a relief expedition to Peking. From June 12th to August 14th the Foreign Embassies, which were situated in a separate part of the capital, were subjected to a regular siege, the most dramatic event in which was the murder of the German Ambassador in Peking, Freiherr von Ketteler.

These events, which were not only "a political crime but also a political blunder," and which were condemned by unprejudiced and enlightened Chinese,[1] naturally made a great sensation throughout the world. But also, as a matter of course, the responsible politicians of Europe felt they must meet them calmly, and that nothing would be gained by magnifying the affair to enormous dimensions. But it was just in this perspective that William II saw it.

[1] In the first rank of these was the famous Juan Shi Kai, who expressed his strong disapproval of this policy from the first, and by this means opened the way for his future career.

THE TRIUMPH OF CÆSARISM

Four years before, during one of his Norwegian journeys, he had made the first sketch of the well-known drawing which was later reproduced as a painting by Professor Knackfuss, in illustration of the so-called "Yellow Peril."

In the Diary for August 5, 1896, this work of art is thus described: "[His Majesty] has brought with him from his Northland journey a sketch for a new picture. It portrays the arts and industries under the protection of the Army. Beneath a Gothic arch stand ideal female forms representing Art and Industry. A threatening cloud is coming up towards them. Fearful hostile forms emerge from it. A Teuton warrior advances to meet the fearful forms."

As a title to the drawing he had put the words: "Nations of Europe, defend your most holy treasures." But the nations of Europe had laughed at it all. It was a new edition of Cassandra's tragic fate—the god-inspired prophetess, at whom an incredulous generation shook their heads:—

> Und sie schelten meinen Klagen,
> Und sie höhnen meinen Schmerz.
> Einsam in die Wüste tragen
> Muss ich mein gequältes Herz.[1]

But they were determined to have their own way! And now all this awful horror had burst upon unsuspecting mankind—"that which I endeavoured to point out to the world, four years ago, in my drawing, 'Nations of Europe, defend your most holy treasures'—because words are so easily forgotten. But my warnings were unheeded. . . .

[1] From Schiller's "Cassandra."

This may prove the beginning of a war between East and West."

In this state of mind it becomes evident that words the importance of which he had never grasped now lost all their meaning for him, and that he worked himself up into an outburst of hate and fanaticism, which produced a most painful impression, not least upon his own people. " The Chinese have overthrown the law of nations ; they have, in a way which has no parallel in the history of the world, disregarded the sacred persons of Ambassadors. It is a crime the more revolting because it is committed by a nation which prides itself on its old civilization.

"You now go forth to fight against a well-armed and cruel enemy. When you come into contact with the enemy, strike him down. Quarter is not to be given. Prisoners are not to be made. Whoever falls into your hands will be at your mercy ! Just as a thousand years ago the Huns, under the leadership of Attila, gained a reputation, by which they still live in historical tradition, so may the German name be known in such a fashion in China that no Chinaman will ever again dare to look askance at a German. The blessing of the Lord be upon you ! The prayers of the whole nation and my earnest wishes accompany each of you. Open the path for culture, once for all." [1]

Immediately afterwards the Emperor of China

[1] From the speech at Bremenhafen (July 27, 1900). The violent expressions in it made several amendments necessary, in which more especially "the Hun passage" was eliminated. Therefore it is not to be found in the revised *Reclam Universalbibliothek* edition of the Imperial speeches.

in a telegram expressed to the Kaiser his deep regret for the murder of von Ketteler, promised to punish his murderers, and requested the Kaiser to take the lead in the work of restoring peaceful relations. The request was rejected by Chancellor von Bülow, who declared to the Chinese Government that the telegram could not be laid before the Kaiser until satisfactory information regarding the fate of the remaining Europeans in Peking was produced, and until the murder of the German Ambassador had been expiated in accordance with the demands of international law and civilization, and in a way which should guarantee that what had happened could not happen again.

From this it was obvious that the Boxer riots had already lost their force, although the siege of the ambassadorial quarter in Peking had not yet been raised; but for the Kaiser the whole affair still wore the fantastic guise of "the Yellow Peril," which could not be subdued without an alliance between all the powers of heaven and earth.

On the last Sunday in July he held a *Seepredicht* [1] on board the *Hohenzollern*—without doubt the best-known sermon he has ever given. As a text he took Exodus xvii. 11: "And it came to pass when Moses held up his hand that Israel prevailed, and when he let down his hand Amalek prevailed." "Who is there who does not grasp the meaning of these words to-day?" said the Kaiser, after having described the scene when Moses, Aaron, and Hur ascended the mountain whilst the battle was raging at its foot. "The pagan spirit of the Amalekites has arisen again

[1] Naval sermon.

in the Far East. With strength and cunning, with fire and sword, men wish to thwart European commerce and European intelligence, to bar the way for Christian morality and the Christian faith. Again God's message rings out to us : ' Choose us out men and go out and fight against Amalek.' A bloody struggle has begun—many of our brothers are already under fire, many others on their way towards the hostile coast. . . . But you who are obliged to remain behind in the home, to which you are bound by other sacred duties—do you hear God's call which goes out to you and which says to you : ' Go up on to the rock, lift your hands towards heaven '? The prayer of the righteous has much power, when it is sincere. We must not only mobilize battalions of warriors, but also a holy militant force of those who pray."

After a long exposition on the power of prayer " which still to-day can hurl the banner of the dragon into the dust and plant the banner of the Cross upon the wall," he concluded thus : " Some day history will describe the struggles of these times. But man sees only what is before his eyes ; he can only say what the wisdom of his leaders, the courage of his troops, the sharpness of his weapons have accomplished. But one day eternity will show . . . how the secret prayers of the faithful were a mighty power in the strife."

The following week saw the appointment of the new Joshua who was to lead the way in conflict with the Amalekites, whilst Israel knelt in prayer at home. The choice fell upon Count Waldersee

—a man who was remarkably suited to the dramatic part now allotted to him on the stage of the world; but the selection was made on purely personal grounds, and he himself afforded a sharp contrast to that Crusade-like character with which official authority tried to surround the expedition. Count Waldersee—as we have mentioned in an earlier chapter—had displayed notable qualities as an intriguer and courtier during the very first months of the Kaiser's reign, when the preparations for undermining Bismarck were already in full swing. "A capital fox face," was Bismarck's short and pithy description of him. "When he comes to visit me, I have a distinct feeling that he is trying to find out . . . if it will soon be time to order a wreath for me." By his marriage with an aunt of the Empress he had early secured for himself "a place in the sun," but his indifferent military abilities had not, however, been able to maintain him there, and several times he had suffered reverses at the hands of Fate, from which a man with such connections ought to have been exempt. Now he had been waiting for many years for a great war which should give him the opportunity of displaying those qualities in the field which he, at any rate—and probably the Kaiser also—thought he was endowed with. At last a war came—not exactly as he had expected it—but still in an extraordinary form, "a collective action on the part of the Powers," as it was called in diplomatic language, an enterprise fraught with incalculable results—the East against the West, according to the Kaiser's opinion.

Therefore he, too, had his great day, when on

August 18, 1900, the Kaiser bade farewell to his "tried Field-Marshal"—an amiable figure of speech which must not be taken too literally, considering this was the first time he had obtained active command in the field. The Kaiser reminded his officers that Waldersee, with the Powers' consent, was appointed as chief of "the united forces of the civilized world," and particularly insisted that the idea of this appointment had emanated from "his Majesty the Tsar of all the Russias, whose power was felt even in the depths of Asia." It rather detracted from the compliment that this statement was immediately met by a protest from the Russian Government, which assured Germany and the world that Count Waldersee had been proposed by the Kaiser, and that Russia and England had agreed to the arrangement in the absence of a better one, and also because they wished to show a fitting consideration towards Germany as the State whose Ambassador had been murdered and which had therefore suffered the greatest indignity from China. The question was unimportant from a military point of view, and is only interesting as a link in the whole of the dubious arrangement, in which Germany was allowed to play the leading part. The fact was that Count Waldersee's effectiveness was completely neutralized by his "subordinates," generals of various nationalities, who very quickly saw through him and made merry over his incapacity. Besides, it was the diplomatists who had most to say during this remarkable "war," which was, in fact, over before Count Waldersee reached China.

The Emperor of China asked for forgiveness in a fresh telegram, and now the Kaiser also was in favour of peace. The stage thunder was over, the only thing now needed was an impressive concluding tableau. It was arranged in the form of a "Penance Mission," which was sent to Berlin, under the leadership of Prince Chun, to ask the Kaiser's pardon. "The Penance Mission," the arrival of which was one of the greatest sensations of the year 1901, performed its task in a manner which, under the circumstances, must be said to be irreproachable. On the other hand, it was unavoidable that the nation was rather sceptical about the propriety of arranging such a spectacle as that of a pigtailed Chinese prince being sent expressly from Pekin to Berlin in order to be conveyed in a stage coach to the palace, and there ask for forgiveness, listen to a severe lecture, and immediately afterwards be taken into favour and made welcome. On the whole, this Chinese expedition, with Count Waldersee and Prince Chun as its two principal figures, is one of the chapters in the recent history of Germany to which the nation felt itself least attracted. Nor did this feeling only arise at a later period—when the facts began to be seen against the background of history. During the affair the great majority of the German Press were unanimously agreed that revenge and civilization were two ideas so diametrically opposed that they could not be mentioned in the same breath; and when the Minister of War, Herr von Gossler, in defence of the Kaiser's utterances, and naturally with his knowledge, made the notorious observation, "What our forces are doing in China now is only in revenge for what the Huns did among us for centuries," there was a general feeling in the nation at large, as well as in the Reichstag, that—to use a moderate expression—a more untenable argument could not well be produced.

The nation bore no ill will whatever towards the Chinese, partly for the very simple reason that the Huns mentioned in the German "Niebelungenlied," with the legendary King Etzel as their leader, have nothing in the world to do with the Huns who appeared under Attila at the period of the great migrations. It was a historical error of unusual dimensions, created by superficial knowledge, heated imagination, and antiquated notions of honour. But, on the other hand, it is easily explicable just at this time, when the Kaiser lived more than ever in a historical atmosphere peopled with monuments, whilst his armies made Germany's name and his own, things of fear in the Far East.

In the autumn of 1900 he laid the foundation-stone of the so-called Reichs-Limes-Museum at Saalburg, in the province of Hesse-Nassau. Here in ancient times was a Roman citadel, fallen into ruins long ago. The spirit of Cæsar came upon him; legions arose from his speech. "Here on this lovely eminence by the Taunus the old Roman castle rises again from its ashes like a Phœnix—a testimony to the power of Rome, a link in the mighty iron chain which the Roman legions laid round their vast Empire, while at the command of a single Emperor, Cæsar Augustus, they forced

THE TRIUMPH OF CÆSARISM

the will of Rome upon the inhabitants of the earth, and opened the whole world to Roman civilization, which descended in blessing upon it, and most of all upon Germany."

These were telling words at the moment, but, unfortunately, quite at variance with the statements of Tacitus. As is known, the tribes of ancient Germania never came under the sway of Roman culture, fortunately for the world, which needed this human element as an independent link in the work of civilization.

But the Kaiser preferred his own history, which he composed at the moment from fragmentary recollections, linked together by the events of the day. In this way he was always able to obtain the picture he wanted at the time. He bridged the gulf which separates antiquity from the present: the "Niebelungenlied" and the Scandinavian sagas from the latest articles in the *Norddeutsche allgemeine Zeitung*. Nor was this all. He made history rise again in fancy dress, as on this occasion, when at his command an antique pageant rose to view—toga-clad Romans, generals and priests, boys crowned with garlands, swinging censers and singing *Salve Imperator*; Teuton chieftains clothed in skins with gaping jaws of beasts to decorate their helmets, armed with javelins and snow-white shields—all to the honour of the great Cæsar who forced his culture upon the world.

He dedicated the museum with three strokes on a stone—the first in memory of his father, the second " to the honour of German youth—the rising generation who will learn in this museum the meaning of a world-empire." The third blow he dedicated to Germany's future—the united work of princes and people, the Army and the citizens, that it may be as powerful, as firm, as united, as commanding as any in the past, and that, as in olden times it was said *Civis Romanus sum*,[1] so in the future it may be said, "I am a German citizen."

Some months later, on January 18, 1901, there came an opportunity of celebrating a new jubilee. Two hundred years had just passed since the Elector Frederick of Brandenburg obtained permission from the German-Roman Emperor of that time to call himself King of Prussia. It was a Hohenzollern family concern, which to some extent affected Prussia, and only in a very limited sense the German nation. But again the unity and greatness of the Fatherland could be proclaimed with jubilation, again the wonderful mission of the monarchy to the nation could be exalted, the reconstruction of the Empire, under the leadership of "William the Great." A Hohenzollern week was arranged at the Court Theatre, where plays, with the history of the Hohenzollerns for their leading idea, were performed seven days consecutively. Royalty played leapfrog boldly over all facts. Kings appeared, not only the two who had been sufficiently glorified already—Frederick II and William I—but also the first Frederick and the two or three Frederick Williams—nonentities who have long been mere names in the book of history, but who, during their lives, had all been more or less imbued with the dream of Cæsarism.

[1] I am a Roman citizen.

It was no wonder, therefore, that the best and soundest wits rebelled, and that a writer in the *Zukunft* gave vent to his feelings in a lengthy article filled with such questions as these: "Heavens! What is the reason for having a jubilee again now? What is there when we look at history between 1688 and 1888? What has Prussia produced? Frederick—William—Bismarck," and the latter not even a Hohenzollern. But, like Frederick II, a man with courage and power to create history. William I, with his hereditary Prussian obstinacy, strove against him, and only step by step did he consent to take his part in the whole as the final link which completed the evolution.

That is history—strong and true, just and merciless, showing no respect of persons—even as it ought to be told. But William II has one measure for princes, even the most ordinary, and another for the rest of mankind, even the most remarkable. Therefore—to mention a characteristic example—he always has been opposed to Bismarck having an equestrian statue, on the grounds that equestrian statues are only for persons of royal descent.

Naturally! The "leaders" of the people must be mounted on horseback all down the ages high above the whole crowd of pedestrians. These latter must be content to tramp on in confidence, making no remark. The nation must suffer and endure in evil days, under the certain conviction that he who rides in front, "responsible to God alone," suffers and endures ten times as much as any single one of the others. It must raise its head like his, trusting in "our old ally," and, above all, it must not forget the well-known words of William II, "I am leading you towards glorious days."[1] Then at last the triumphal procession will march once more through the *Siegesallee* as on that radiant June day in 1871.

The Avenue of Victory!

The name itself sounds like a blast of trumpets. It was inspired by the idea of Cæsarism and carried out in plastic art with that strange Cæsarlike determination which constantly shows itself in William II.

The *Siegesallee* was in a way his "bridal gift" to the German nation: the history of Brandenburg, Prussia, and Germany expressed in marble—an avenue of thirty-two marble statues, ranged in a double row, extending more than five hundred yards in length and over twenty-five in breadth.

To begin with it was not particularly easy to make a choice—"not so much with regard to the princes as with regard to those who assisted them in the execution of their work." These words were spoken by the Kaiser in a speech delivered in 1901 on the completion of the great work. He flattered himself that within the limits of the task in hand he had allowed every single artist the necessary freedom in the performance of his work; and he was proud and happy in the knowledge that it had actually been accomplished by none but Berlin artists. "It shows," said he, "that the Berlin school of sculpture has reached a level of excellence which could not have been higher even

[1] In the original: Herrlichen Zeiten führ Ich euch entgegen.

in the days of the Renaissance. . . . I may tell you already that the *Siegesallee* is making an overwhelming impression on foreigners. All over the world an immense respect for German sculpture is to be found." Here, again, was one of those Imperial illusions with which reality had nothing to do.

All over the world the *Siegesallee* is quoted as a hideous warning, and hardly anywhere has judgment been more severe than in Germany itself, where people are familiar with its history and know what enormities have been committed in the execution of the work. Thus it is a well-known fact that while the faces of some of the earlier princes have been hunted out of old engravings as far as it has been possible to find such in the archives, others are simply taken from theatrical and operatic representations.

"Goethe said that the actor should learn from the worker in art; now it is the other way round," wrote the well-known art critic Karl Scheffler in 1901. "Cloaks picturesquely draped, bold silhouettes of helmets, commanding gestures, doughty attitudes . . . crowns, artillery boots—to put it shortly, a waxwork exhibition! Everything exactly to order. A trouser button is just as carefully treated as an eye; a coat of mail casts a deeper shadow than a head." But the criticism does not get as far as Cæsar. He has his very decided opinions on art in general and sculpture in particular, and he rejoices that the art of sculpture —at any rate, in Berlin—has been for the most part untouched by the so-called "influences" and "tendencies," and therefore has retained the power to educate the people, which ought to be the object of all good art.

"God grant that German sculpture may always remain at its present height of perfection, and that my grandsons and great-grandsons may have equally great masters by their side."

CHAPTER XIV

DISAPPOINTMENTS

NOTWITHSTANDING the less pleasant features of the expedition to China, it would be idle to deny that it had its importance in the recent history of Germany as the last link in the work of welding Army and Navy into one organic whole.

During the jubilee year it had been the Kaiser's regret—to which he had given expression more than once—that the Navy had no memories of battle to which it could look back in the same way as the Army. But now this was no longer the case. The marine forces (who happened to be in China before the dispatch of the other detachments, which arrived too late to take any part in the operations) had, from a military point of view, done excellent work, and displayed a courage and resource concerning which there was only one opinion among their foreign comrades. The British Admiral, Seymour, had commanded, "Germans to the front!"—an order which seems to have made an indelible impression on the Kaiser, and which he often took the opportunity of recalling. Therefore he was able with no exaggeration to say to his sailors on their return in 1901: "From now onwards there can be no doubt that the Army and Navy are one. They can mutually rely upon each other. The one expresses its respect towards the other." Seen in the light of the Navy Act of 1900, with its huge programme extending over a space of fully sixteen years, these words have an increased importance. Quite apart from the politics of the day, they mark the accomplishment of a purpose which he had had in his mind ever since he was a young Prince; certainly not with much result, but with indubitably good intentions, a purpose of which the Great War was one day to show the consequence. In this one respect something had really been accomplished; but just at this time, when he was about to reap, as it were, the reward of his exertions, an incident occurred which had a deep effect on him, at the same time throwing a light on certain aspects of political life in Germany which made a painful impression on the rest of the world.

During a visit which the Kaiser made to Bremen on March 6, 1901, a young man named Weiland, who was standing among the spectators in the street, threw a piece of iron in his face, with the result that the Kaiser sustained a scratch on the side of his nose, four centimetres in length. The injury was completely healed within a fortnight. It was proved that Weiland was insane, and, when speaking to the President of the Reichstag, who, on behalf of the Assembly, had expressed his sympathy, the Kaiser described this senseless attack as "the action of a person obviously deranged."[1] But nevertheless he could

[1] In the original language: Der Tat eines offenbar blöden menschen.

not get rid of the idea that the young man had been led away by some bad influence. He expressed the same opinion in still stronger words in a letter to the President of the Prussian Second Chamber, at the same time attaching far-reaching importance to the occurrence.

"The outrage in Bremen," he writes, "shows what confusion reigns in immature, youthful heads. It is obvious that respect for Crown and Government is diminishing more and more. In this direction things have become worse during the last ten years. Respect for authority is wanting. The fault lies with all classes of the people. Instead of serving the general interests of the nation, every man pursues his own private interests. The criticism of the measures taken by the Crown and the Government assumes the most cutting and offensive form. The result of all this is confusion and demoralization of the young." These words were taken generally as being an answer on the Kaiser's part to the Agrarians and the Conservative part of the Press, who had lately attacked him on account of his stay in England at the time of Queen Victoria's death. They aroused a considerable sensation, which increased when the Kaiser practically repeated his words to the Reichstag and Landtag. The newspapers discussed the affair at length with a most painful want of tact; and in a way which one would have thought inconceivable in a country like Germany they asserted that the attempt had plainly had an injurious effect on the Kaiser's mind.

At this he immediately protested in the most positive manner.

"I have read everything that the newspapers have written about my supposed condition of mind since the affair at Bremen," he said in an address to a deputation from the Prussian First Chamber. "But there is nothing more mistaken than to suppose that my mind has suffered in any way whatever through this affair. I am exactly the same as I have always been. I have not become either dreamy or melancholy." Here the Kaiser, who had Weiland's piece of iron in front of him on the table, paused, pointed to the missile, and continued: "I am in the hand of God, and I will not allow even such events as these to divert me from the path in which I deem it my duty to go. During my journeys I meet with all classes of the population, and I therefore know very well what is thought and said about me in the nation. But if any one thinks that incidents such as this will alarm me and affect my future actions, he is very much mistaken. Nothing will be changed."

The words could not be misunderstood. The German nation had once more been told exactly where it stood. But it seemed, nevertheless, as though the Bremen affair had unnerved him, more than he himself realized, or, at any rate, more than he would admit; and when he was inaugurating the new barracks at Kupfergraben, near Berlin, for the Kaiser Alexander Regiment, five weeks after the attempt, his agitated condition again betrayed itself:—

"Like some strong castle, the new building which has now been assigned to you raises its walls by the palace, which it must be your first endeavour always to protect. The Kaiser Alexander Regiment is required to be, as it were, a bodyguard night and day—always ready to strike for the King and his house, and, when necessary, to sacrifice life and limb on the redoubt. And if ever such a time should come again "—here the Kaiser made a brief allusion to the events of 1848—" if there should arise in this city a rebellion against its ruler, I am convinced that the Alexander Regiment will crush out all insubordination and disobedience towards the King and keep disorder within due bounds."

And in a special address to the officers of the regiment he added the following words, which in this time of war have a special interest:—

"I am firmly convinced that the officers of the Alexander Regiment will always be equal to their task, and will train up their soldiers to sacrifice life and limb for King and Fatherland if it should be needful. The consciousness of this makes me feel assured that even if we should be surrounded by enemies on all sides we would be victorious everywhere, and this because of our most powerful Ally the gracious God in heaven, who, ever since the time of the Great Elector and the great King,[1] has always been on our side."

The speech made a great sensation, both in public and private circles, and was widely interpreted as an infallible proof of mental depression.

But, as was very justly pointed out at the time, it was quite unnecessary to draw such conclusions. Even before he had been struck by Weiland's piece of iron, "the picture of civil war," as Harden said, "was always before his mental eye." He

[1] Frederick II.

had called on the Prussian Guard to defend him against the " gang of traitors," and enjoined on the young soldiers to shoot down father and mother if they were commanded so to do. In short, there was not a new note in the whole speech.

Instinctively all thoughtful people asked one another yet again: What will be the end of this? Will it answer in the long run for foreign countries, who do not know and cannot know German affairs as we do, and who therefore lack the necessary qualifications for judging the value of the Imperial speeches, to harbour the belief that Germany lives under the shadow of civil war? Ought it not to be made clear how far the majority in the Reichstag sanction the actions of the Kaiser, his conception of the world—his *Weltpolitik*, his impulsive eagerness to impress his sovereign will upon public opinion? If the Reichstag sympathizes with him—very well, then ; he stands within his right, and no criticism need meddle with him further. If not, we must return to the practice which obtained at the time of William I, when there was always a responsible authority behind the Imperial words.

Admirable suggestions, which people made vigorous exertions to realize later on. But for the time being there was no one who dared to take the first step, a characteristic sign of the long-suffering character of the German temperament.

In the meantime a very important change took place in the highest office of the State.

The Chancellor, Prince Hohenlohe, had retired from public life in October 1900, at the advanced

DISAPPOINTMENTS

age of eighty-one. His last parliamentary victory had been the adoption by the Reichstag of the Navy Bill, which passed, on June 12th of the same year, by 201 votes to 106. On this occasion the Chancellor made a speech which, on one point, constituted an indirect protest against the official view of the subject. Every one knows it has been long held as a dogma in Germany that it was the Kaiser who had aroused interest in the Navy throughout the German nation, and who had finally carried the day in spite of the shortsightedness and waywardness of his countrymen. We have pointed out in an earlier chapter that this view, which the Kaiser himself has tried to instil into the public, is not entirely correct. This fact, however, should not prevent recognition of the Kaiser's work. But neither should the nation be forgotten. This was the view which Prince Hohenlohe urged at the moment, and on the basis of his own personal recollections since 1840, he maintained that "the desire for a German Navy had in reality issued from the German nation."[1] Although he inserted the observation very diplomatically in a subordinate sentence, it is not less noteworthy on that account. There is something of an independent assertion in it—a distant echo from the days of youth, sixty years back, before he was drawn into the official system, which clipped his wings and reduced him to "Uncle Chlodwig" by the pitying indulgence of his countrymen.

[1] In the original language: das Drangen nach einer deutschen Flotte recht eigentlich aus dem deutschen Volke hervorgegangen ist.

Hohenlohe's resignation did not meet with any opposition on the part of the Kaiser. Quite the contrary.

"During the last weeks" (of his time in office), he noted in his Diary, "several things occurred [1] which impressed me with the conviction that a change in the person of the Chancellor would not be displeasing to the Kaiser." Hohenlohe, who thought that it was better to anticipate the event than to be overtaken by it, decided to retire "earlier than he had originally designed." His keen perception did not mislead him. The Kaiser graciously received his resignation, "and my departure was accomplished in a most peaceful way, without any feeling of injury on either side." The nation and the Reichstag received the news of Hohenlohe's retirement with the same indifference which they had displayed when he took office. Popular opinion did not suggest any particular man as his successor, and the question had really been decided by the Kaiser in his last political conversation with the retiring Chancellor. "I was agreeably surprised when he at once mentioned von Bülow," writes Hohenlohe in his Diary. "He is, at any rate for the moment, the best Chancellor to be had." Immediately afterwards a telegram was sent to Herr von Lucanus to arrange the necessary formalities, and then von Bülow slipped into the position of Chancellor with a simplicity which showed that the German nation was still in a

[1] Among other things Prince Hohenlohe strongly advised the Kaiser against appearing in the dress of a Roman emperor at the inauguration of the Reichs-Limes Museum, to which advice the Kaiser reluctantly yielded.

primitive position with regard to political power and authority.

The new Chancellor had many qualities suited to his high position. He was a man in the prime of life, and did not belong, as did the former Chancellor, to a period which lay a generation and a half before the Kaiser's own. He had grown up in a definite political atmosphere, and had early come within the magic circle of Bismarck's genius, who, in von Bülow's father, had one of his most capable and zealous fellow-workers. Notwithstanding a difference in age of ten years, he had been a personal friend of the Kaiser from his youth. He had enjoyed a liberal, even superior, education, improved by studies and travels; and he had also a thorough knowledge of practical administration extending through many years— latterly in the capacity of Secretary of State for Foreign Affairs and as acting Chancellor under Hohenlohe on several important occasions. No intrigues were needed to push him forward as Chancellor, nor any camarillas to support him. But, on the other hand, he had no firm footing either in public opinion or in the Reichstag, although his powers were universally recognized and he was looked upon as one of the finest speakers in the Assembly. He had already established his fame in this respect in 1897 by his famous phrase about Germany's need of " a place in the sun "—an expression which the Kaiser has quoted so often that millions of people, both in Germany and outside, have long ceased to entertain the slightest doubt as to its Imperial origin.

The new Chancellor came into office at a very difficult moment. But it was not internal affairs only which gave cause for anxiety. In the field of foreign policy also there were forces at work which threatened to make deep rifts, especially in the relations between Germany and England, which were already considerably strained.

The German nation had, through a foreign policy the instability of which was nowhere more severely criticized than in Germany, gradually worked itself up into such a state of indignation towards England, on account of the British course of action in South Africa, that it almost assumed the character of general hatred. " It cannot now be open to doubt," says Count Ernst zu Reventlow in his work on Germany's foreign policy,[1] " that those accusations of inhumanity which were directed against British operations in South Africa went far beyond the mark. The appalling miseries in South Africa, which fell particularly upon the Boer women and their children who were interned in concentration camps and died there, were horrible and painful facts. But people went too far when they described them as the result of inhumanity. . . . Nor could the British soldiers justly be accused of any want of courage or of any propensity to cruelty."[2] But at the moment indignation overshadowed everything else, and if the German nation, during the last months of 1901, had known what we now know of German foreign policy, it would hardly have felt itself much edified.

[1] Deutschland's auswärtige Politik 1888-1913.
[2] Cf. Sir Valentine Chirol's article "The Origin of the Present War" (the *Quarterly Review*, 1914, pp. 414-49).

The Kaiser, the Chancellor, and the German Foreign Office, in opposition to the nation, desired a closer connection with England, and in October 1901, following a suggestion on the part of Germany, informal preliminaries were discussed between them respecting a treaty of alliance by which the two Powers would have guaranteed to respect each other's possessions all over the world, excepting those in Asia. Germany had no interest in placing herself on the side of England against Russia in a possible collision in that part of the world, but she intimated at the same time that there was another Power upon whom England could confidently depend as an ally—namely, Japan. On the side of the English, it was pointed out as a singular thing that Germany desired the alliance to be extended to include North and South America as well, where it was well known that she did not possess a single colony. But Germany made an earnest assurance that this was just a proof of the disinterestedness of her policy. England did not feel able to take this view; and besides this she was afraid lest a concession on her part to the German policy, the tendency of which was directed against the Monroe Doctrine,[1] might some time in the future lead to a conflict with the United States. But from a European point of view, too, the proposed alliance had one great weakness as far as England was concerned. By guaranteeing to Germany what this State pos-

[1] Of 1823, called after the famous President James Monroe (1817-25). It is to the effect that the United States will not permit any intervention in the internal affairs of the American States.

sessed in Europe at the time, England would
have settled the question of Alsace-Lorraine in
Germany's favour, and thereby have incurred the
abiding hatred and wrath of France. Under these
circumstances England did not feel herself able to
agree to the German proposals and the intended
alliance fell through. In the place of it, England
shortly after entered into the famous alliance with
Japan, which within a few years was to have
such a decided importance.

There is a statement of the Kaiser's, mentioned
in Hohenlohe's Diary for 1900, which at the first
glance makes it difficult to explain why he sought
England's friendship with such perseverance, not
only then, but on earlier occasions as well. Speaking
in French, the Kaiser said: "I like England
and the English, but I have no confidence in their
politics."[1] The explanation lies close at hand,
however. It is the German *Realpolitik* which
shows itself, divested of all its outward conventionality,
or, as a French politician once expressed
it: "The Kaiser always offers to be your friend
against some one else. Without this your friendship
is of no value to him." The assertion is
historically correct, and, more than that, this attitude
on the part of the Kaiser was an outcome
of the Imperial temperament. A foreign policy
which is constantly dictated by nervousness must
necessarily abound in advances and assurances in
different directions, while at the same time disappointment
and bitterness must increase with each
new rebuff. This was particularly the case on this

[1] J'aime l'Angleterre et les Anglais, mais je me méfie de leur politique.

occasion. As long as these negotiations lasted the German Press was practically quiet. The British negotiator, Sir Valentine Chirol, who in those days went in and out of the Wilhelmstrasse, received a definite impression from the Chancellor that both he and the Kaiser wished to be on good terms with England, and that there was nothing they disapproved of more than the uncontrolled attacks on England, which we referred to earlier, in connection with the agitation at the beginnnig of the new century. But now, when the negotiations for the suggested alliance came to nothing, the German Press suddenly started on a most violent, united attack upon England.

Sir Valentine found this behaviour on the part of the Press, which was supposed to be inspired by the Foreign Office, so contrary to the impression he had received during his stay in Berlin that he felt himself obliged to ask Baron von Holstein for an explanation.

It came by telegram and ran thus: *Wir haben einen Korb bekommen.*[1] This was official Germany's last bitter admission that once more she had received a repulse from England, and at the same time it marks the Kaiser's last attempt to draw England into a position with respect to Germany which, according to British opinion, would have ended by reducing her to what has been called " a maritime Austria." From now onwards the path was clear for German naval policy down to the Great War. The Navy Acts of 1906, 1908, 1912, and 1913 followed one

---

[1] German colloquialism, meaning: Our proposal has been rejected,

another like beads on a string—all engineered by
the agitation we have sketched in outline, and
the leading idea of which was that the naval
policy and the *Weltpolitik* were to form one
organic whole, the object of both being that no
decision of importance should be taken anywhere
in the world without the opinion of the German
Emperor first being heard.

But still the crowned heads in both countries
continued to pay visits to each other for several
years, and to assure each other of their personally
friendly feelings, and it need hardly be said that
it was William II who chose the strongest and
most spontaneous words.

One of these utterances deserves to be specially
mentioned—in the first place because it was made
immediately after the hostile display towards England, and secondly because it has a practical value
to-day.

It was a tribute to the Prince of Wales—the
present King George—who, by his famous journey
of over 60,000 miles, had helped to " weld together
these distant parts of the British Empire and their
loyal inhabitants, and to incorporate them into the
Imperium Britannicum, of which it can be said
that within its boundaries the sun never sets."

CHAPTER XV

THE *METEOR* AND OTHERS

SIMULTANEOUSLY with the events sketched in the last two chapters there arose another reason to make official Europe become more and more suspicious of the Kaiser's assurances of peace.

At the end of August 1898 the present Tsar sent out his famous Peace manifesto, which led to the summoning of the so-called First Hague Conference. It recommended on broad lines that lasting peace should be secured for the nations of the world by a systematic limitation of the enormous armaments which even in time of peace were such as to threaten the nations with economic ruin. It is easy enough now, in the light of recent events, to smile at this Conference, and at the benevolent monarch who took the first step in the matter. But it is a fact that, while the British Government, under the leadership of Lord Salisbury, who several years before had advanced the same idea, expressed their entire sympathy with the Russian suggestion, it was simply dismissed in Germany. It may be mentioned also as a significant fact that Professor Stengel of Munich—a teacher of international law, who on the first suggestion of the Conference showed himself to be one of the most persevering agitators against the scheme—was appointed as the official representative of Germany at The Hague, together with Professor Zorn of Berlin, who was also a decided opponent of it, particularly with regard to the idea of compulsory arbitration. About the same time the Kaiser, in a speech made at Wiesbaden, recommended the keen-edged sword as the best guarantee of peace. All this very naturally attracted attention. The only person who seemed to think everything all right was the Kaiser himself, who, with his unique power of deluding himself into every kind of error, naturally never doubted for a moment that all official Europe felt exactly the same as he did.

"When I succeeded to the throne," said he in a speech in 1902, with a new variation of the same expressions which he used towards the Army at the time of the ten years' Jubilee, "foreign countries met me with a deep but unwarranted mistrust, believing that I was striving after the laurels which are the reward of war. In the face of this mistrust it became my task to convince foreign countries that the new Emperor and Empire intended to devote their strength to the maintenance of peace. This task needed a long space of time for its fulfilment. . . . The German Empire is now far from being considered a danger to peace. On the contrary, people have learned to look upon us as its greatest bulwark."

It is not to be wondered at that, with such inability to comprehend anything in the nature of facts, he experienced one political disappointment after another and saw great things accomplished contrary to his Imperial will. In 1901 the Triple Alliance began to break up, as far as Italy was concerned, and afterwards that policy was initiated which led to the Tripoli War in 1911, and to the final rupture between Italy and Germany in 1915. In 1902 the alliance between England and Japan was concluded which in 1914 was put to the test, and which in the case of Germany has led to the loss of Kiao-Chao. Involuntarily, Bismarck's half-jesting words of warning came to mind: "Kiau-Chau! one must get accustomed to the name. It may turn out to be a long-drawn-out *caout-schouc* [1] for us." All this was disquieting and irritating, and the Kaiser felt obliged to speak more often and more clearly than ever before.

First it was America to which he turned—"a land which, ever since the time when he was Prince, he had tried to familiarize himself with by reading and careful study"—to quote an official author—"and which he has always regretted that he has not been able to visit." By means of sundry telegrams and speeches on various occasions, during the 'nineties he had tried to cultivate American friendship, but during the war between Spain and the United States in 1898 things looked critical for a time on account of the conflict which arose between the distinguished Admiral Dewey and the commander of the German Squadron off the Philippines.

This feeling of dissatisfaction might now be removed, and as a suitable opportunity the Kaiser made use of the fact that his yacht, the *Meteor*,

[1] *Caout-schouc*—French for indiarubber.

which became so famous later on, was to be launched at State Island. His brother, Prince Henry, who had returned the previous year from his expedition to China, and who had been praised in a fashion which was out of all proportion to what he had done, had to set off again—and with the tendency to exaggeration always present, it followed as a matter of course that the public had to be prepared for surprises.

The Kaiser had given his brother the advice one would have least expected from that source: " Keep your eyes and ears open, and your mouth shut ! "

As the Kaiser's representative and official spokesman on all occasions, it was naturally no easy task for the Prince to take the last part of the advice literally. He was obliged to rise and speak time after time, and he assured his hearers constantly " that he had come to America in order to show that Germany wished to stretch out a hand of friendship across the ocean—nothing more nor less." Or, as one of his American friends expressed it: " He has come to learn and observe ; to become acquainted with our country and people, our industry, our ships and machines, and our gigantic shops." The beginning was an excellent one. Prince Henry telegraphed the news of his arrival to President Roosevelt, and at the same time took the opportunity of inquiring after one of Roosevelt's little boys, who, unfortunately, was obliged to be in bed at that moment. " And permit me, in addition, to congratulate you and the Americans on this the birthday of Washington."

The remark was worthy of his Imperial brother—the great recollector of the birthdays of the living and the dead. But such he must be, for as he said of himself before his departure for China, he had gone forth " to preach the gospel of your Majesty's exalted person." Roosevelt forgot to return thanks either in his son's name or in Washington's, and confined himself to greeting him on his own behalf and on that of the American nation on the occasion of his arrival.

Miss Alice Roosevelt, the President's eldest daughter, who had been commissioned to christen the *Meteor*, was more spontaneous. With a refreshing lightheartedness she scribbled off at the breakfast table the following telegram to the Kaiser :—

Meteor has been successfully launched. I congratulate you and thank you for your courtesy to me, and send you my best wishes.

The example was catching, and with a seriousness which proved that the primitive republican virtues which had existed from the time of Washington and " Citizen " Lafayette had not yet died out in the States the Prince was assured by almost every single speaker that he had reason to feel proud of his reception in America. He was informed that he was liked and respected for his own sake.

" With your ability you would, as a citizen of the United States, certainly have attained to the rank of Mayor," declared a high State official in a speech in honour of the Prince—" perhaps even to that of chief of the naval administration."

On the other hand, the German-Americans were beside themselves with joy.

"Incredible numbers of them appeared everywhere," writes the Prince's American friend. "He asked them how they were getting on, and among the answers he got, he was most pleased with those to the effect that the Germans were good American citizens. They could not show their loyalty to Germany better, he said, than by also being loyal citizens of the United States."

The words were ordinary, without originality, which was not, indeed, their object. But the Byzantine Press on both sides of the Atlantic was already getting on the scent of history, and with the conscientiousness suitable to the situation, the German-American Press considered no incident too insignificant to be transmitted by cable.

"The Secretary of State [the American friend] was wearing the jacket of the Imperial Yacht Club to-day, while the Prince was in ordinary civil dress." "The Prince-Admiral has inherited his father's winning smile; that smile will take all hearts by storm for him in America. . . ." "The breath of history is already about us." Of course. This journey, which went at lightning speed in a Pullman car across the American continent, had quite another object than that of making Prince Henry acquainted with "country and people, industry, ships, machines, and gigantic shops." It was to preach "the Imperial gospel" in the New World as it had been proclaimed long ago in the Old. This was admitted among officers —by Admiral von Tirpitz, who plainly declared:

"We expect an improvement in the relations between the two great nations, who have no conflicting interests in any part of the whole wide world." Chancellor von Bülow expressed his absolute sympathy, and could not see even in the most distant future that there was any point "where the Germans and Americans can cross each other's way."

But the Americans themselves were not so charmed, and when the journey was well over, and the Prince at home again, things began to come out even in correspondence to German papers. "In political circles outside the Press everything stands just where it did before the Prince's arrival. . . . In distinguished American circles the opinion is general that a more important occasion ought to have been selected for the Prince's tour."

This view really asserted itself so forcibly even during the visit that it gradually affected the Prince himself, and cooled the fervid expressions which were as natural to him as to his brother on all festive occasions.

But to the Kaiser this journey was an event which ought to be remembered for all time; and in token of the historic and unchanging friendship between Germany and the United States, he astonished both the world and the American nation by presenting America with a bronze statue of Frederick the Great, for which he requested President Roosevelt to choose a suitable site in Washington.

But Prince Henry's journey to America had another object still. This was to strengthen national consciousness in the German-Americans, and take them out of the dilemma in which they found themselves with regard to their new and their old home. "Both these facts," said a semi-official writer fourteen years ago, "may one day prove to be of the highest importance for Germany, and people will then fully appreciate the value of the German Emperor's exertions and his infallible foresight."

The words have a certain value to-day as an indication of the end in view, even though they have been deprived of some of their truth through unfortunate mistakes, as well as by the actual force of circumstances. As far as the commercial side of the visit was concerned, it was pointed out from the very first, with praiseworthy soberness of mind, that nothing of the kind was ever intended. "Trade and commerce, export and intercourse are not under the influence of feelings and high-flown speeches. Therefore it would be a mistake to suppose that the friendly relations which the Kaiser has established with the United States could be specially advantageous to our trade and export."

Far more important than either the political or economic objects of his visit was, however, its psychological side, the principal one in the Kaiser's view, and that which made him dispatch his brother on this pilgrimage to secure the favour of the Yankees. Wrapped in an entirely mediæval conception of empire, he had become a religious enthusiast—something akin to Otto III,[1] out of whose dreamy mind there constantly arose the most magnificent castles in the air, and thus his interest

[1] Germano-Roman Emperor, 980–1002.

in the American community was not purely intellectual. He was bound to it first of all by his British descent, secondly by his mechanical and practical interests, and finally by those qualities which go to make some of his most characteristic weaknesses—his restlessness, his love of sensation, and his untiring passion for establishing records.

His individual gifts and talents, and the surroundings in which he grew up, combined to give him that marked self-assertion which the Americans develop naturally, placed as they are in the midst of a community of self-made men, where energy and skill open undreamed-of possibilities, and where the highest honour and distinction lie within every man's reach as far as his abilities go. The representatives of money met him on an equal footing, in virtue of "the almighty dollar," which in the last resort is able to counterbalance a Hohenzollern. The Pierpont Morgans, Vanderbilts, Armours, and all the other princes of finance raced with him at Cowes and Kiel. He was not capable of impressing them because there was no bridge to connect his antiquated world of thought—the atmosphere of pedantry and uniforms, parade and regulations, in which he continually moved—with their period. On the other hand, he received an overwhelming impression of their independent world because he instinctively felt the connection between this community and that of industrial Germany, a Germany of which he himself knew nothing, in spite of all the Hohenzollern traditons. At first he no more understood this phenomenon than he had understood the social side of the Labour question. But when Capitalism began to assert itself in the German community also, and its representatives were able to procure themselves all the material comforts which had hitherto been reserved to the nobility by birth and the military profession, the situation changed. Before either he himself or official Germany, became aware of it, one of the pillars of the altar and the Throne was distinctly shaken and " the new aristocracy," as it has been called, had entered upon the scene, imperious and defiant, and nowise hampered by considerations of any kind.

The phenomenon is not a new one. The history of Rome during the last hundred and fifty years B.C. reveals it, from the point of view of antiquity. It occurred in England during the eighteenth century, and in France it practically coincided with the first half of the Second Empire.

In Germany—as we have mentioned in an early chapter—it was more particularly the outcome of the gigantic financial disturbance which arose after the Franco-German War; but in spite of that unfortunate economic crisis, out of which Stoecker tried to create a clerical and social-religious policy, with the support of young Prince William, capitalism itself was only temporarily stunned. In the course of half a generation it rose again stronger than before, in sympathy with industrial and commercial developments, and the wonderful new discoveries which were being made in the departments of electrical and chemical industry. Life assumed a different aspect. Everything went on at greater speed; desire both for pleasure and convenience increased, and invention hastened to satisfy it.

William II was caught in the swirl of this development in spite of his exclusive traditions, his military enthusiasm, and his strictly orthodox conception of life, with all their corresponding rules of etiquette, which were to him inviolable as a Divine ordinance.

The following words were written during the celebration of the Emperor's silver wedding in 1906: "During the early years of his reign William II devoted himself mainly to military matters, and his only recreation was hunting. In accordance with this he associated with the nobility alone. But the moment the monarch began to turn his attention to yachting and motoring there arose a change. Only a few of our nobility could afford to have their own yachts and motor-cars, and it was therefore necessary for our monarch to make acquaintance with representatives of the German moneyed class." On closer investigation, it appeared that the members of this class, who as a rule are descended from the Maccabees, were willing to devote their means to the patronage of art and literature—to found charitable institutions and to fill the museums with rare treasures. William II did not content himself by merely showing his gratitude in the forms of titles and orders. He was of opinion that the gentlemen who had placed themselves so promptly at the service of the ends he wished to advance were worthy to associate with him personally, and he opened his doors to them.

At that moment the social alteration was accom-

plished and a new age came in. " What has
hitherto been regarded as German character and
German virtue is disappearing," observes a dis-
tressed author, " and with the gentlemen of the
new age there arises a new conception of life
which would hardly have kindled inspiration in
an Arndt and a Schenkendorff.[1] The old nobility,
which, religiously, politically, and socially, was
knitted to the previous generation and to that
system which the Kaiser defended on every occasion, in total opposition to his present behaviour,
withdrew more and more from the Court and
retired as the " Junker party " to their estates,
where, to speak with the *Vorwärts*, they expressed
Simplicissimus sentiments. In their place the new
aristocracy came in—parvenus with brand new
titles, clever and pushing men with strong lungs,
as was right and proper in a generation where the
main thing was to shout as loudly as if in a Stock
Exchange and wave company prospectuses and
quotation records above one's head as though they
were a gilded shield.

It was this development in the recent history
of Germany which took place about the middle
of the 'nineties, at the same time that the Kaiser
began to proclaim a *Weltpolitik* as his great aim.
It was connected with the desire for colonies and
the naval movement which have been sketched
in an earlier chapter, and from its very nature it
was aggressive without being definitely bellicose.

But the Kaiser here, as in so many other
instances, stood with one foot in each camp—

[1] Famous poets associated with the German rising against
Napoleon.

because he wished to be both autocrat and democrat, the Hohenzollern monarch by the grace of God, and the workman's Kaiser, the apostle of peace, and the partisan of the " keen-edged sword "—to put it shortly, because he could not realize the deep contradictions between the old Prussian kingdom and the modern German Empire, and thus try to establish some harmony between them ; therefore as time went on his policy became more and more nervous, instead of becoming, as might have been expected, more temperate and composed as the result of a more comprehensive and far-seeing view.

In one way Prince Henry's tour to America was an official confirmation of the fact that the new age had made its entry, and that the German Empire intended to fly her standard at the foremast of the *Meteor*.

There was almost a warning underlying the name, which might have made an orthodox Prussian of the old school hesitate. But the Messrs. Bodensteins, and Huldschinskys, Lüderitzes and Itzenplitzes, Markuses and Loewes, and all the rest of those typical representatives of money, who have transformed modern Germany into a pocket edition of America, without the elements of greatness and independence which, in spite of all faults and shortcomings, lie at the root of the American community—these wealthy gentlemen were troubled just as little by superstitions as by ethical considerations.

The only one who, in spite of all, did not seem to suit his surroundings was the Kaiser himself. At Aachen, for instance, in the summer of 1902, some months after his brother's American tour, he described the new Germany and its ideals in the following words:—

"Far and wide our language spreads beyond the seas, far and wide extends the influence of our science and our research. There is no work in the field of new investigation which is not first produced in our language, and not a new scientific thought which is not first grasped by us and subsequently adopted by others. The foundations upon which our nation rests are simplicity, the fear of God, and the high moral attitude of our forefathers. . . . I place my whole Empire, my whole people, my whole Army, represented by this field-marshal's baton, under the control and protection of Him of Whom the great Apostle Peter has said, 'Neither is there salvation in any other,' . . . and who said of Himself, 'Heaven and earth shall pass away, but My words shall not pass away.'" And as an aspiration which did not only apply to the city where he was speaking at the moment, but to the whole Empire, he concluded with the confident words: "I drink to the prosperity of the city of Aachen, fully convinced that the words which I have spoken will fall on fruitful soil."

CHAPTER XVI

NERVOUS SYMPTOMS

DURING the years 1903 and 1904 comparatively little was seen of the Kaiser. He made, indeed, some sensational speeches from time to time and some remarkable observations, of which the most interesting, psychologically, was his religious confession of faith, contained in a letter to Admiral Hollman, a document which gave rise to a lengthy controversy in the German Press, and which was also discussed abroad.[1] Among his political speeches there was one in particular which aroused dissatisfaction abroad. It was delivered in Hanover. The Kaiser has never been able to speak in that city without touching on the memory of Waterloo—the great traditional bond between England and Germany. Now he referred to the same subject again, and, among other things, let fall the remark that it was the Hanoverians, together with Blücher and the Prussians, who had saved the English from annihilation in that ever-memorable battle.

[1] The letter, which is reproduced verbatim in the third volume of the Kaiser's speeches (*Reclam Universalbibl.*, nr. 4803–5), is supposed, according to the publisher, to be without doubt due to the influence of the Rev. Dryander, principal Court preacher of the Kaiser.

With the exception of this unconsidered remark, for which there was no possible cause, and which had not even the advantage of being true, he exhibited on the whole a more prudent policy, both towards England and the other Powers, than people had been accustomed to during the last few years. In one way, however, it was a work of necessity—firstly, because conditions in general demanded a certain prudence if Germany at all intended to strengthen her position in Asia; and, secondly, because it became more and more evident that the ranks of Germany's friends were thinning.

A conflict between Germany and Venezuela, immediately after Prince Henry's visit to America, came as the first check, and destroyed the entire impression both of the visit and the Imperial gift, which in any case had not given particular delight. In order to appease feeling, the German Ambassador in Washington, von Holleben, was recalled from his post and replaced by Speck von Sternburg. The new Ambassador, who went over to America in 1903, began by making the assurance that " it is very important for the Kaiser to show the Americans that he stands in friendly relations with them. Nor is there any place in the world where the Monroe Doctrine is respected so much as in Germany, where it is regarded as the most valuable guarantee for peace in the Western hemisphere." The general public in Germany could not, however, rid themselves of the notion that several mistakes had been made by the Government both about America and about the other Powers. This view was even advanced in such a loyal newspaper as the *Frankfurter Zeitung*, as well as in the Opposition press, while the Radical and Socialist speakers took it up freely in the Reichstag.

" It cannot be doubted that our policy regarding the Boer War was not particularly successful," wrote the Frankfurt organ. " And what are our relations now with regard to the United States? We can see here how little importance need be attached to royal visits. Prince Henry was received everywhere with acclamation, but it now appears that the cannonade at Maracaibo,[1] of which no satisfactory explanation has yet been given, is enough to cause an explosion of ill-will against Germany." And, with a true discernment of the real cause, the journal continued: " We are far too busy cultivating friendships all over the world. We want far too many friends, and—as Herr von Vollmar said—we are far too pushing in our advances towards them. The result is that we forfeit those friendships we already have. In the end we shall not have one sincere friend, but find distrust on every side."

What was very important for the Kaiser was a permanent understanding with Russia, whose policy towards China, and in a less degree also towards Japan, became more and more defiant in the course of the summer and autumn of 1903. There is reason to believe that the object of the German policy was to make Russia more disposed to agree to the new commercial treaty with Germany, which, after the alteration of the

[1] An allusion to the German bombardment of the Venezuelan port of that name.

German tariff in the direction of Protection, was decidedly less favourable to Russia than the one which had been adopted whilst Caprivi was Chancellor. But even towards the end of 1903 these negotiations were far from being complete. Russia's representatives did not seem to be in any hurry, while the Russian papers plainly asserted that Germany's policy aimed at sowing discord between Russia and England by officially supporting Russia's attempt to obtain a peaceful solution of the difficulties in Macedonia at that time, and at the same time privately encouraging Turkey to resist the Powers' demands in this connection. We mention these observations, not as a proof that Germany was really playing a double game, but because it is necessary to draw attention to them as showing the general distrust which prevailed as to the honesty of German policy.

As far as the Kaiser himself was concerned, it was obvious that all his interest regarding his attitude to Russia was centred in the Russian policy of extension in Eastern Asia. In spite of the humiliation of China and the effective concluding tableau of " the penance Prince," he had not yet completely shaken off his fear of the " Yellow Peril." Professor Knackfuss had long ago completed his work of art, and the Kaiser very naturally had presented it to the Tsar, whose " powerful arm reached deep into Asia," and who therefore, more than others, ought to have his attention directed to the danger which was threatening. That he was also equal to resisting it the Kaiser did not doubt for a moment, and when war broke out between Russia and Japan, in 1904, he expected a speedy and complete victory in Russia's favour.

A succession of circumstances — among them being the facility with which Russia reduced her troops in Poland to a minimum and sent the rest to Manchuria, while Russian deserters across the German frontier were handed over to the military authorities of their own countries, and German steamers were sold in great numbers to Russia— served to strengthen the general impression that verbally or actually, directly or indirectly, there existed some alliance between Russia and Germany, directed, not only against Japan but also against England. The matter has an interest beyond the actual moment, and must be reckoned as a factor in judging the events which made it natural for Japan to place herself in 1914 in the ranks of Germany's enemies.

Notwithstanding this benevolent attitude on the part of Germany, which even brought some difficulties upon the Government in the Reichstag, events took their undisturbed course towards the breakdown of the Russian policy in the Far East.

The Kaiser followed the development of events with the greatest attention, and expressed his sympathy on several occasions. "Russia's grief is Germany's grief," he telegraphed in the spring of 1904, on receiving the news that the battleship *Petropaulovsk* had struck a mine and gone down— a sentiment which all humanity could share, among other things because the gifted painter Vereshchagin was drowned on the same occasion. Later in the year—when the Viborg Regiment, of which the Kaiser was honorary colonel, was sent out to the East—he telegraphed to the regiment, wishing them all success in their opportunity of meeting the enemy and of sharing the honour of fighting for their country. He also expressed the hope that good fortune would follow them.

These sentiments were just as strong at the beginning of 1905, and on the fall of Port Arthur, on January 2nd, he hastened to decorate General Stössel with the order *Pour le mérite* in recognition of his heroic bravery. Later on it was unfortunately proved that General Stössel's conduct during the siege of Port Arthur had been scandalous, and that he had surrendered the fortress much too early—conduct which a court of justice in his own country found it necessary to punish by ten years' imprisonment. It was inevitable that General Stössel's fate should place the Kaiser in an unfavourable light, as a man who acted far too impulsively under the impressions of the moment, without giving himself time to make any inquiries whatever as to the real facts ; nor did it improve the case that he bestowed the same decoration on General Nogi, the conqueror of Port Arthur. On the whole, the Kaiser's disappointments over the progress of the Russo-Japanese War were so many and so personal that it is conceivable that pure despondency caused him to utter the disparaging observations about the Russian Army which we have already mentioned, even if the form they took was unjustifiable.

The year which opened in such a dramatic way was, however, to be exceptionally full of surprises.

In March he made one of his most remarkable speeches at Bremen—a mixture of supposed self-abnegation and passionate defiance—not exactly new in idea, but still so amazingly expressed that it was very naturally made the subject of much comment both at home and abroad.

"When I came to the throne," he said, "after my grandfather's great work was achieved, I swore a soldier's oath that, as far as lay in my power, bayonets and cannons should remain at rest; but I swore, too, that the bayonet must be kept sharp, the cannon loaded, and both in good condition, so that neither jealousy nor envy from without might disturb us in the cultivation of our gardens or in the decoration of our beautiful homes. I have pledged myself, on the ground of the experiences of history, never to strive after the vanity of a world-wide domination. For what has become of these so-called world-wide Empires? Alexander the Great, Napoleon I, all the great captains of war, after wading through seas of blood, left behind them nations crushed beneath the yoke who rebelled again at the first opportunity and brought their Empires finally to their fall. The world-wide Empire which I have imagined is characterized by this, that, above all things, it shall enjoy the most absolute confidence on all sides as a quiet, honest, and peaceful neighbour; and if ever a German Empire or a Hohenzollern dominion should be known in history, they should not be founded on the conquests of the sword, but on the mutual confidence of neighbours, striving towards the same end."

He further maintained that the German Army,

practically speaking, had now reached its highest
possible state of perfection, and that therefore it
was now the turn of the Navy. Now at last the
Navy was filled with the same spirit as the Army,
while every German warship that was launched
was one more guarantee towards peace on earth.
" Our adversaries will be so much the less disposed to stir up strife against us, while at the
same time we shall be looked upon as a desirable
ally."

After a few remarks about the rising generation and the Fatherland, he expressed his firm
conviction that " our Lord and God would not
have given Himself such pains over our German
Fatherland and its people if He had not some
great thing in store for us." He concluded with
the following passage : " We are the salt of the
earth ; but we must also show ourselves worthy
to be so. Our rising generation must learn to
make sacrifices, to renounce all that does not tend
to good, and to avoid everything which has crept
in from foreign countries. So may it one day
be inscribed on the German nation what is written
on the helmets of my 1st Regiment of Guards,
Semper talis (' Always the same '). Then all will
look upon us with respect and some even with
affection, and we shall be able to stand with our
hand on our sword-hilt and the shield before us on
the ground and say, *Tamen* (' Come what will ')."
Nine days later—March 31, 1905—these remarkable words received a practical illustration on the
occasion of the Kaiser's visit to Tangier. After
the attitude which the Imperial Chancellor, von
Bülow, had adopted with respect to the Franco-

British Morocco agreement of April 8, 1904, during a debate on the question in the Reichstag, this sudden visit of the Kaiser to Morocco became an international event of the first importance. The Chancellor had alleged that the German Government had no objection to the agreement, as it was in no way inimical to German interests, and when Count Reventlow remarked that it might be advantageous to Germany to create friction between the other Powers, von Bülow diplomatically replied that, "at any rate, it would be unwise to proclaim it from the housetops." But that is just what occurred. The Kaiser landed at Tangier and proclaimed to all the world that, in view of Germany's important commercial interests in Morocco, he had decided to place himself there as a safeguard for the sovereignty of the Sultan and the independence of the country, and in order that a free Morocco might be open to the peaceful competition of all nations, without monopoly and without restrictions.

This action was of course interpreted as a challenge to France and the two other Powers—England and Spain—who had contracted the Morocco agreement a year before, and if there was any one who still entertained any doubt about the matter he need only read the comments of the German Press on the Morocco affair. The articles, which were inspired by Wilhelmstrasse, briefly declared that in reality the German Government took up the same fundamental attitude towards the Morocco agreement as it did in 1904—that is to say, that it raised no objection to the agreement itself, but it considered that a mistake had been made on the part of France by her not informing Germany of the treaty before it was signed. It was the wish of Germany that France should make amends for this mistake by joining with Germany in a conference on the Morocco question as far as it also concerned the other Powers. In other words, a purely formal question was here raised in the most dangerous and defiant manner, and it was evident that a retreat was bound to be made in some quarter or other if Europe were not to face a most critical situation.

It lies beyond the limits of the present volume to enlarge upon the well-known events which during the first days of June 1905 brought about the resignation of the French Secretary of State for Foreign Affairs, M. Delcassé, as a member of the Rouvier Ministry. It is sufficient to say that all over the world this incident was regarded as an open acknowledgment on the part of France that she had been worsted in the dispute with Germany. Such was undoubtedly the case. Yet it was no more than a stage victory, won because of the chance circumstance that France at the moment was in an isolated position, because her Russian ally in the Far East had suffered the defeat which both Delcassé and William II had thought impossible at the outset.

There can hardly be found a more striking evidence of the short-sightedness in the so-called leading circles of Europe than that this sudden action on the Kaiser's part should have been considered a remarkable result of political shrewdness, and that it should be prophesied, even in England, that the Kaiser's action in Morocco had secured Germany a leading position in European politics for many years to come.

Long before the outbreak of the Great War the logic of events had proved the emptiness of this assertion, and there is hardly a more striking proof of this than that the only thing now remaining of the Imperial Morocco policy is the title of Prince which was granted to von Bülow towards the end of the summer 1908—*Bernhard der Glückliche* [1] as his countrymen called him—during the first exuberance of joy at Delcassé's having been obliged to retreat.

But it was not enough for the Kaiser to carry his point with a high hand. The fact had to be repeated again and again so that everybody should know that no one might dare to cross the path of Germany, and that the Kaiser's advice and wishes must be consulted in all decisions of importance. A new and admirable opportunity for proclaiming this opinion offered itself on October 26, 1905—the hundred and fifth anniversary of Moltke's birth. A statue of the great soldier was unveiled in Königsplatz, in Berlin, and in the evening there was a banquet at the palace.

The Kaiser spoke :—

"Let us consecrate two glasses to this day—one to the past and its glories, in sincere thankfulness to Providence which in former days gave the great Emperor his paladins. . . . The second glass I dedicate to the future and the present. You have seen, gentlemen, how we stand in the world. Then—powder dry, sword keen, eyes on the goal, muscles taut, and down with all

[1] Bernhard the happy.

pessimists ! I fill my glass to our people in arms." [1]

There was such violence of feeling and such distinctness of expression in this outburst that no impartial outsider could entertain a doubt of its fundamental sentiment. It was the policy of nervousness proclaimed to all the world, not by chance but as a system—a policy always on the verge of declaring hostilities, under the sense of being surrounded by enemies on every side.

But a living, working nation cannot exist permanently in such an atmosphere of excitement, without reaction setting in sooner or later. It came in the autumn of 1905 in the form of an interpellation in the Reichstag, the result of a more than usually defiant speech made by the Kaiser in Breslau—a speech full of martial recollections and imperious demands. It was in this speech that he let fall the well-known words which have been so often quoted : " I will endure no pessimists. The man who will not join with me in the work, out with him ! Let him go and seek another Fatherland elsewhere."

The Liberal Party and the Socialists, and even the Moderates, felt that things were going badly, and during the interpellation in the Reichstag words were spoken with unusual sharpness. " We have reached," said Bassermann, leader of the National Liberal Party, " a period of journeys and speeches, telegrams and overflowing amiability in every direction. Our policy has no dignity or stability.

[1] In the original : Das Pulver trocken, das Schwert geschliffen, das Ziel erkannt, die Kräfte gespannt und die Schwarzseher verbannt.

The plans which are made are afterwards thrown into confusion by violent hands. Foreign States watch us with attention and distrust." A more distinguished Liberal Member said: "It is high time that all these empty speeches and clashing of swords were put a stop to," and one of his colleagues supported him by remarking that "there is nothing more dangerous in home policy than a personal autocracy, and it becomes even more dangerous in the case of foreign policy." The Socialist Herr Wollmar made the general remark that "it is a matter for astonishment abroad that a nation so highly cultivated as the Germans should remain in such a state of political subjugation," while Herr Spahn—leader of the Moderate Party—without criticizing the Imperial remarks, suggested the unusual step that the foreign policy of the Empire should be placed under constitutional control, under the guidance of a Commission for Foreign Affairs, headed by Bavaria, an arrangement which was included in the Constitution, but which has never been carried into practice.

This debate showed the real feelings of the nation, and it would be an easy matter to emphasize this by bringing forward contemporary evidence taken from pamphlets and books, as well as from articles in magazines and in the daily Press. But even on this occasion no decisive change took place. Then suddenly Wilhelm Voigt, an old unknown shoemaker with a stormy past and a by no means military appearance, exposed the whole vulnerable side of that Imperial policy of uniforms to which the Reichstag had tried to put an end in vain. It was long since people had laughed so heartily in Germany as on the day that the old cobbler appeared in a mock captain's uniform at the head of a detachment of soldiers, of whom he had calmly taken command in the street, arrested the local authorities of the town of Kopenick, and possessed himself of the municipal coffers.

Things like this could happen even in a country where a uniform was the "alpha and omega" of life, and where the Emperor never wearied of reiterating the fact that he was "determined to have brave and stalwart soldiers in his Army and no mockers." Goethe's words were true, and the cobbler Voigt proved them in practice, "From the sublime to the ridiculous there is only one step."

CHAPTER XVII

AN INTERVIEW AND ITS CONSEQUENCES

THERE is hardly anything more characteristic of the abnormal political conditions in Germany than that the crisis which was so obviously approaching still held off for nearly two more years. When it finally came, it was the Kaiser himself who precipitated a commotion in Germany which has had no parallel in the last fifty years.

On Wednesday, October 28, 1908, the *Daily Telegraph* published an article with the title "The German Emperor and England." It took the form of "a personal interview" between the Kaiser and the writer of the article, who described himself as "a retired diplomatist." With a true estimation of the journalistic value of direct speech, the author made the Emperor appear in the first person. The words poured from his lips. The reader feels that they are sentiments which have been kept back for years and which now at last burst triumphantly through their bonds.

"You English are mad, mad, mad as March hares. I have declared to you repeatedly and emphatically that it is one of my dearest wishes to live on good terms with England. Falsehood and prevarication are foreign to my nature. That you mistrust me and will not believe me I feel and resent as a personal insult. A considerable section of your newspapers warns the people of England against accepting the hand I hold out, and insinuates that in my other hand I hold a dagger. I can only repeat again and again that I am the friend of England, although here I find myself in a minority amongst my countrymen. The prevailing sentiment among large sections of the middle and lower classes of my people is unfriendly towards England. I strive with all my power to improve our relations, and in spite of all, you persist in regarding me as your archenemy.

"During the South African War Germany was full of the most hostile feeling towards you. Both publicly and privately the whole current of opinion was directed against England.

"But what did I do? Who put an end to the Boer leaders' circular tour, the object of which was to bring about a European intervention against yourselves? I did.

"These men were received with acclamation in Holland and in France, and the German nation would have liked to have woven garlands for them. But I declined to receive them, and at once the agitation stopped and England's enemies obtained nothing.

"When the struggle in South Africa was at its height the German Government was invited by the Governments of France and Russia to join with them in putting an end to the war. The moment had come, they said, to humble England in the dust. I replied that Germany would never lend her aid in bringing about the downfall of England, and that she never would be drawn into a policy that could bring her into conflict with a sea Power of England's rank.

"In the archives of Windsor Castle there still lies the telegram in which I informed Queen Victoria of the plans of her enemies and of the answer I had given them.

"Nor was that all. During your Black Week in December 1899, when disasters followed one upon another, I received a letter from my revered grandmother which betrayed her deep sorrow and affliction. I not only returned a sympathetic reply, I did something more. I bade one of my officers procure for me the most exact account he could obtain of the number of combatants in South Africa on both sides and of the actual positions they occupied. With these figures before me, I worked out what I considered to be the best plan of campaign for you under the circumstances, and sent it with the approval of my General Staff to England. This document is likewise among the State papers at Windsor Castle. My plan was in all essentials the same as that which was so successfully carried out by Lord Roberts.

"Would an enemy of England behave thus?

"But you will say: 'The German Navy is a menace to England.' No! We need a powerful fleet to protect our commerce and our other interests. The circle of these interests is constantly enlarging. We must be prepared for those eventualities in the Pacific Ocean which may arise sooner than many people believe. The rapid advance of Japan and the awakening of China show us how grave are the problems which confront European power in the Far East. When the German and British squadrons are fighting together on the same side, England will rejoice over the fact that Germany had a strong Navy."

This is the substance of the famous "interview," which was at first regarded in Germany as something in the nature of a hoax. But when it was transmitted over the world by Wolff's Agency and reproduced in the *Norddeutsche Allgemeine Zeitung* two things were made clear: the wording was correct, and it was the Kaiser's wish that his remarks should be circulated as widely as possible.

There is no reason to refer in greater detail to the unique sensation which this interview created throughout the world. But as far as Germany was concerned, it is no exaggeration to say that it was like an autumn storm—a gale which swept over the land and aroused opposition among all ranks and professions, even in the Army itself.

Never had there been such resistance—not to say such actual rebellion—against the Kaiser as arose on this occasion, both in speech and writing. For more than a week the newspapers, without regard to party, raised one united chorus of lamentation over that personal rule which had caused Germany to be exposed in such a way, and there was only one opinion to be heard—namely, that effective measures must be taken against this political evil which threatened to lower the very idea of monarchy itself.

"The treasure of monarchical feeling which the Emperor William I bequeathed to his successors is undoubtedly very rich," wrote the Liberal organ *Die Post* in an article which may be quoted as a specimen of the average opinion; "but even the greatest inheritance may be squandered if it is administered in an irresponsible manner." Carried on the topmost wave of indignation, Maximilian Harden went so far as to ask straight out if the Emperor intended to abdicate the throne. "He must not cherish any illusions," he added. "All his subjects are against him now."

In the Reichstag, where Prince Bülow found himself in a difficult position, not least because the Imperial interview had been exposed to a series of peculiar misfortunes on its way between the various State authorities, words were no less bitter.

The manuscript, according to the *Norddeutsche Allgemeine Zeitung*, had been submitted to the Kaiser in a handwriting that was practically illegible. His Majesty, who at the moment happened to be at his well-known royal hunting lodge, Rominten, in East Prussia, ordered it to be sent to the Imperial Chancellor. The Chancellor, who was spending a few days on his estate at Norderney, on the North Sea, sent it on straight to Wilhelmstrasse, without looking at it. Here the Minister for Foreign Affairs was not at home —he was taking his holiday at Berchtesgaden, in Tyrol—and neither in the "Press Office" nor "the political department" was there any one who took the trouble to examine it. After having undergone this, to say the least of it, summary treatment, considering its Imperial origin, the document was returned to the Chancellor, who now saw less necessity than ever for looking at it.

He contented himself with giving it the usual endorsement which is signed on all the Chancellor's dispatches, *Erledigt—B.*,[1] and after that no one thought more about it until it appeared in the columns of the *Daily Telegraph*.

The whole thing produced a distinctly painful impression of irresponsibility; nor could it be denied that there was a certain comic side to the situation. If for no other reason, it was imperative, on purely formal grounds, that the Foreign Office should be safeguarded by "constitutional guarantees." There appeared no other course open to the Chancellor but the tendering of his resignation. He had now been over eight years in office, and had experienced to the full both its delights and its drawbacks. His health was failing and the leisure of private life appealed to him as it did to few, surrounded as he might be by works of art, by books and outward comforts, in his splendid villa at Rome, or refreshing his tired brain in the salt sea breeze on the beach at Norderney. But on second thoughts he felt, in spite of all, that it would not be quite loyal to leave the Kaiser at a moment like this—when he stood practically defenceless before a whole nation which was "just bursting with indignation and shame," as a German writer put it. Von Bülow therefore went no further than to inform the Kaiser that on certain conditions he was willing to remain in office —after having actually tendered his resignation.

He informed the Reichstag of the position, and added:—

"It is my firm conviction, and one to which

[1] Dispatched (Bülow).

I have come during the strain of these days, that the Kaiser will in future observe, even in private conversation, that reticence which is necessary in the interests of a uniform policy as well as in that of the authority of the Crown. If this were not the case, neither I nor any of my successors could accept the responsibility."

The high tone in which the discussion was opened by the Chancellor was maintained throughout the debate, and it was justly admitted, even by British observers, that none of that dignity was lacking which befits the National Assembly of a great people in a situation which, from its very nature, must be painful.

But the attacks on the Crown increased rather than diminished in violence, and some days later the Socialist Heine made a speech which, by its audacity, deliberately encouraged rebellion, but which nevertheless was not referred to by a single word from the ministerial bench.

"The Kaiser has formed the habit of speaking on all possible subjects," said the member in question. "He speaks on science, little dreaming how men of science shake their heads; he speaks on art, but does not realize the smile that goes round in art circles; he speaks on politics—and about that we have heard enough. Thanks to the Kaiser, national unity has been re-established, but it is a unity of indignation."

The attitude taken by the Government party was due as much to the personal character of this attack as to the perfectly sound judgment on which it was based—namely, that personal rule, according to the Kaiser's conception, was an impossible thing, for the practical reason that no human being can be familiar with all subjects, in all departments of knowledge, in such a highly specialized age as our own. It was difficult enough to be an autocrat in the days of Frederick II, and even Bismarck's giant constitution was on the point of giving way more than once under the burden of the Chancellorship. The work of Chancellor was now three or four times as heavy as it had been in his time, and yet the Kaiser wanted to be his own Chancellor—as well as everything else. It was obvious that this could not go on, and it was hopeless to bring forward anything in defence of such a system. Therefore the Government party kept silence, both to avoid a crisis in the Chancellorship and to prevent what a Conservative speaker called " an open declaration of war between the Crown and the nation."

Curiously enough, this violent constitutional storm left no traces whatever on the Kaiser himself. While the nation was eagerly waiting for a word of some kind from him to confirm the Chancellor's statement, persistent rumours began to spread hinting that the relations between the Kaiser and his Chancellor were more strained than before. At the same time the newspapers occupied themselves in recording the Kaiser's private diversions, which the nation at that moment was inclined to regard as something in the nature of a defiance.

From Rominten the Kaiser had gone on a hunting expedition to Bohemia with the Austrian Heir-Apparent, Archduke Francis Ferdinand, who, with his wife, less than six years later, was to be immortalized in the double tragedy at Serajevo. At the moment the Kaiser was staying with his friend Prince Fürstenberg at his magnificent castle of Donaueschingen, in Bavaria, where were also Count Zeppelin and several other gentlemen. Here hunting still went on, and in the evenings there were various forms of amusement. A theatrical company from Frankfort-on-the-Main, and a troupe of variety artists from the Chat Noir in Berlin, appeared amidst tremendous applause. During his visit Count Zeppelin gave a demonstration with one of his airships. The Kaiser decorated him with the Black Eagle, and made a speech declaring him to be " the greatest German of the twentieth century."

But his Majesty was not only taken up with the actual doings of the moment. In a few weeks' time he was to receive the oath of allegiance from the new recruits at Kiel. Some fresh saluting regulations were necessary, and Admiral von Holtzendorff published the following instructions from the Kaiser, with orders that they were to be carefully practised so as to be employed on his Majesty's arrival.

" His Majesty the Kaiser has commanded that the cheers on each ship shall be absolutely simultaneous, at the exact moment that the caps are raised high in the air. On the command ' Three cheers for,' the flags must be run up. At the same time the right hand of each man on parade must be removed from the rail and carried to the edge of the cap. On the first command to cheer, the signalling flags are to be dipped ; the cheer is then to be uttered, while at the same instant the caps are to be raised a short distance into the air by extending the right arm at an angle of about forty-five degrees. As soon as the first cheer has subsided, the caps are to be brought to the front of the body by bending the arm at the level of the chest. The same procedure is to be observed at the second and third cheers, the only difference being that after the third cheer the caps shall not be brought to the front of the body, but shall be smartly replaced on the head, after which the right hand shall be returned to its position on the rail."

The nation felt itself more and more left in the dark, and new rumours continually cropped up.

What was the meaning of this behaviour on the Kaiser's part?

Was there anything in the report that Prince Fürstenberg was to be appointed Imperial Chancellor?

"That is impossible," was the reply of those people who knew better—" if for no other reason than that Fürstenberg is an Austrian citizen."

Or perhaps the Kaiser again contemplated taking a Chancellor from the Army?

In this connection General von Loewenfeld's name was mentioned; he was chief of the 9th Army Corps in Hanover—the same corps that Caprivi was commanding when he was called to the highest office in the State in the manner we have already described.

No one knew anything. The only thing certain was that the agitation in the nation was becoming more and more disquieting, and it finally aroused such serious anxiety in Court circles that the Kaiser

AN INTERVIEW: ITS CONSEQUENCES

decided to have a personal interview with the Chancellor.

This event, which the public was informed of beforehand, took place on November 17, 1908, a date which the majority of the people at first expected would be a landmark in German history on the way towards constitutional self-government.

The official communication, published in the *Reichsanzeiger* on the same day that this important interview took place, gave no grounds for such an assumption. It briefly informed the public of the fact that the Chancellor had had an hour's conference with his Majesty the Kaiser, and had drawn His Majesty's attention to the sensation created in the German nation by the article in the *Daily Telegraph* and to the reason of this sensation. Further, he had given the Kaiser a detailed account of the attitude which he—the Chancellor —had considered it his duty to adopt during the proceedings in the Reichstag. After this the official communication continued as follows:—

"His Majesty the Emperor received the statements and explanations of the Imperial Chancellor with great seriousness, and expressed his wishes in the following terms: Notwithstanding the exaggerated nature of this public criticism, which he felt to be most unjust, he would consider it his highest Imperial duty to guard the stability of national policy, while fulfilling his constitutional responsibilities. In accordance with this, His Majesty the Emperor gave his assent to the statements of the Imperial Chancellor and assured Prince von Bülow of his continued confidence."

But as the old proverb says, "It is an ill wind that blows nobody good."

If the crisis had not come to a head in the columns of the *Daily Telegraph* at the end of October, it would have done so in the *Century Magazine* in the beginning of November. During a two hours' conversation with a prominent American journalist the Kaiser expressed himself in his usual open-hearted way. The German Foreign Office, to which the article had been submitted, was of opinion that it ought to be published in a magazine of good standing, and the choice very naturally fell on the *Century Magazine*, though the author had originally written his interview for the *New York Times*. But after the affair with the *Daily Telegraph*, Wilhelmstrasse felt such a dread of any more Imperial interviews that all the cables were instantly set in motion to prevent a new sensational bomb from bursting over Germany and the world.

Nevertheless, it was pure accident which decided how far any of their measures took effect.

The interview had long ago been produced in proof sheets in the *New York Times*, and copies of it had passed through several hands in America. A couple of corrected proofs had even made the journey across the Atlantic to England. The *Century Magazine* had the interview in type ready to go to the press, and though it had been moderated from its original form, the paper felt that out of deference to the reasons put forward by the German Foreign Office it ought to abandon the idea of producing this unique journalistic sensation, which undoubtedly would have beaten all records of the *Daily Telegraph*.

AN INTERVIEW: ITS CONSEQUENCES

However, that did not help matters. The *New York World* took up the sensation and published a version of the interview, which was recognized as right in all essential points, but which lacked the personal flavour which would have been its chief qualification for success. Now it only served to show that with regard to Japan the Kaiser was still in dread of the "Yellow Peril," while towards England he displayed a feeling of ill-will which stood in marked opposition to the views which he had expressed in the interview for the *Daily Telegraph*. But this was not the first time he had contradicted himself.

CHAPTER XVIII

BEFORE THE GREAT WAR

AFTER the Imperial declaration of November 17th, it did not take long for the loyal people of Germany to settle down again. This state of things was a proof of the nation's notable lack of political instinct, and its willingness to be satisfied with words. The Kaiser's declaration, indeed, stated that he agreed with the views which the Chancellor had expressed in the Reichstag; but, so far from admitting that the criticism had any justification, he considered it on the contrary to be simple injustice and exaggeration. In complete accordance with this attitude of mind the Kaiser made no promises of any description. He was free at any time to withdraw what he had said, and to assert the same views as before, without any one being able, with even a semblance of justice, to reproach him for having gone back on his word. Also, on purely practical grounds, it was wise to let a certain time go by before he again appeared as the autocrat "responsible to God alone."

In consequence of current events his speeches during 1909 were mainly concerned with private matters. These speeches were all very quiet, especially the first, which was indeed the most difficult one—namely, the welcome of King Edward and Queen Alexandra on the occasion of their visit to Berlin in February 1909, three months after the national tempest we have sketched in the preceding chapter. His speech on the occasion was absolutely irreproachable. For once we hear nothing of Malplaquet and Waterloo, the hope of a mutual brotherhood in arms in future, or the joint task of the German and British Navy in the struggle for European civilization. He merely expressed the usual assurances of friendship which are required on occasions of this kind, adding that he recognized in this visit " a new guarantee for the peaceful and friendly development of the relations between the two countries."

Some weeks later, in a speech on the first centenary of the institution of the Prussian War Office, there came an opportunity for him to take a more exalted tone. This temptation also he resisted, although his feelings took him beyond the most ordinary set phrases. He gave honour where honour was due, in recalling the memory of Scharnhorst and Roon—the only epoch-making War Ministers in Prussia during the nineteenth century. He did not so much as mention his grandfather, and only referred to his great-grandfather Frederick William III as the official originator of the War Office, without using any of those superlative adjectives which history does not justify, and which on other occasions he had lavished so freely on this unremarkable and indeed unattractive individual.

Later in the year he showed the same moderation

when speaking before the Tsar as he had shown before King Edward, and in the speech from the Throne at the opening of the Reichstag in the autumn of 1909 there was a remarkably subdued tone, with no high-flown language of any sort, and above all no demands for grants towards the Army or the Navy. He pointed out that Germany's distant possessions were developing satisfactorily, and that a large part of those expenses which the Empire at first had been obliged to defray, were now borne by the colonies themselves. Commercial treaties had been concluded with England and Portugal. To put it shortly, the entire political horizon was peaceful, or, as he expressed it in the speech from the throne: " In order to secure to the German people undisturbed and adequate opportunities for development, my Government continually exerts itself to cultivate and strengthen peaceful and friendly relations with the other Powers."

All this bore undoubted witness to the significance of the crisis of 1908—and showed that the Kaiser could be induced to adopt an attitude of greater self-restraint if the nation would really risk anything to obtain it. But, on the other hand, an incident occurred in 1909 which was calculated to arouse anxiety, because it showed that the Kaiser had learnt nothing from the Algeciras disappointment in 1906, when the emptiness of Morocco's imaginary claims of the preceding year was exposed to the world, but that he henceforward held the opinion that the policy of strong words led most surely to the goal.

In the autumn of 1908 Austria-Hungary, contrary to all expectations, annexed Bosnia and Herzegovina. This event made a general sensation throughout the world, and for nearly six months threatened to bring about war between Austria and Serbia. A breach between these two countries would, in the opinion of all authorities, be synonymous with a European war. The Powers of the Triple Entente were most seriously offended, because the action of Austria-Hungary practically implied the abrogation of one of the most essential clauses in the Berlin Treaty of 1878, and enlarged the sphere of Austria's interests in the Balkans. To Russia, who was still exhausted after her war with Japan, Austria's action was nothing less than a defiance. But as Russia had no power to support her case, Serbia to all intents and purposes stood alone. The result of this was the famous Serbian Note of March 31, 1909, in which the chief point was that Serbia formally and actually acknowledged the justice of the Austro-Hungarian annexation of Bosnia and Herzegovina, and promised to adopt in future a more conciliatory attitude towards her great neighbour.[1] A more decisive victory could not have been gained by the Austrian Foreign Office, chief of which at that time was Count Aehrental. But even so it was clear that he would not have been able to force his policy through if Germany had not supported him in a way which really left Russia no choice between a hopeless war and an unquestionable diplomatic defeat, of which

[1] It was one of Austria's strongest accusations in the note of July 23, 1914, that Serbia had for several years completely disregarded the note of 1909.

alternatives she chose the latter. The Kaiser, moreover, made no secret of the matter when he visited Vienna, a few weeks after the publication of the Serbian note. On the contrary, he proclaimed loudly to all the world that during the crisis which had just been dealt with in so satisfactory a manner he had placed himself " in shining armour " by the side of his ally. This was a speech which could not be misinterpreted, and it furnished a new proof that German foreign policy continued in the same path which it took in 1905. The Kaiser evidently intended in the future to add his important weight to the scale in accordance with that previous remark of his, which we have quoted, that no great decision should be made in the world without the German Emperor's consent.

From a psychological standpoint this behaviour was quite natural, although there were weighty objections to it from the political side. The Kaiser was now fifty years of age, and time had not modified to any appreciable extent the original features of his character. The self-willed child, of whom Dr. Hintzpeter complained that he was not amenable to the moral and spiritual influences of parents or teachers, had now become an arbitrary middle-aged man without any of those qualities which characterize the thoughtful politician or the skilled diplomatist. He was neither far-sighted, calculating, nor persevering, and the whole of his art consisted in staking all upon one card—and confiding in his good sword. This was of course an excellent policy while any one could be found who would allow himself to be imposed on by it. But there is nothing really powerful about it, and its final end was long ago expressed in the old proverb, "The pitcher goes to the well, till it comes home broken at last." For this same reason the Kaiser had no sympathy with the proposals put forward by England between 1906 and 1912 for establishing a "naval holiday"—a reduction of the enormous naval armaments which were so great a burden on both German and British finances. Germany consistently refused to join, and in the Reichstag, Chancellor Bethmann-Hollweg made a statement which indicated the fundamental view of official Germany on the subject, in a manner which left no room for doubt. "There is an old saying which still holds good," he said, "that the weak are an easy prey for the strong. When a nation will not or cannot go on spending enough on its armaments to maintain its position in the world, it sinks down to a lower level and ends by becoming nothing but a spectator on the stage of the world. The vital strength of a nation can only be measured by its armaments." The new Chancellor, who proclaimed so clearly that Germany intended to go her own way, regardless of any peaceable desires or representations on the part of others, had succeeded Prince Bülow in the summer of 1909. He was born in 1856, and was, as has been mentioned, a member of the "Borusser Corps" at Bonn during the Kaiser's student days. His official career had been continuous and painstaking, and he had risen step by step to the position of Minister for Home Affairs. In this capacity he had come into close relations with von Bülow, who frequently made use of his assistance, and allowed him to appear on his behalf in the Reichstag. The gradual progress of development had made the position of Minister for Home Affairs practically that of Vice-Chancellor, and there is no need to point out that this circumstance largely contributed to bind Bethmann-Hollweg to von Bülow, and make him his natural successor in office. As a political speaker the retiring Chancellor was polished and witty, with a certain satirical gift which never failed to succeed even with an opponent. The strong point of the new Chancellor lay in his thoroughness and genuineness; and his sound, somewhat academic speeches were always listened to with attention. But at bottom he had a more sensitive nature than most people imagined; and there are probably few contemporary politicians whom Fate has used so hardly, or who have so inexorably been made the victims of a system with which they have hardly a single moral or intellectual point of sympathy.

In an Imperial speech delivered at Königsberg on August 25, 1910, we meet this system again, the same as it was in earlier autocratic speeches. Here there are no more restraints, no more reservations. It is proclaimed openly and exultingly that in this city the Great Elector made himself " sovereign-duke of Prussia in his own right; here his son Frederick I was crowned, and thereby brought Brandenburg into the position of a European State; here Frederick William established his authority and paved the way for the greater Frederick II " ; and above all: " Here once again my grandfather, in his own right, placed on his head the crown of Prussia. He received it—as he himself asserted—by the grace of God, not through Parliaments or popular assemblies. He, therefore, looked upon himself as an instrument chosen by Heaven, and in that spirit he discharged his duties as Lord and Ruler." What was here said of the grandfather naturally applied to the Kaiser himself also. They were the same ideals which he had always preached, and which he proclaimed yet again in defiance of 1908.

But Königsberg was not only the cradle of Prussian absolutism. It was also the place of Germany's resurrection after her hour of distress under Napoleon. Full of enthusiasm, the Kaiser dwelt on the memory of his great-grandmother, Queen Louisa, " Prussia's good genius," whom he idealized in a fashion which history no longer recognizes as legitimate. He stated that what should be learnt from Prussia in the time of her distress was simply " that in view of the enormous strides our opponents have made, our armour must be without flaw. Our peace depends solely on the fact that we are armed." All this was just a new variation of his earlier words, and of the views expressed in the Chancellor's speech—childish and primitive conceptions of things, empty assertions modified neither by time nor changing circumstances.

It was in this frame of mind that he made " the Panther's leap " [1] in the spring of 1911. The result was a summer full of international agitation,

---

[1] The popular designation for the dispatch of the warship *Panther* to the port of Agadir in Morocco—an incident which the world first became aware of when the *Panther* was lying in Agadir's roadstead.

which several times brought Europe to the brink of a world-war. The utter shortsightedness of his policy was now evident. The trump cards of 1905 and 1909 were no longer of any service. The Triple Entente was an indisputable fact, the might of which left no way open save retreat. The Morocco Agreement of November 4, 1911, was a public confirmation of this. From there the road led, through the two Balkan wars, straight to the events of the summer of 1914.

With the material now available we can only indicate the main lines of the picture presented by Germany during those three years which lay between the Morocco Agreement and the outbreak of the Great War. Against this background the Kaiser shows out more strikingly than before because he obviously stands more and more alone —a singular prelude to the shadowy existence he was to lead during the war itself.

M. Jules Cambon, formerly French Ambassador at Berlin, in the first part of the French " Yellow Book," which covers the time between March 17 and November 22, 1913, has given us a study of national psychology which is of great value for the comprehension of German feeling during the years immediately preceding the war. It may be objected that the picture is one-sided, and it is fair to add that its accuracy is disputed in German quarters. But it is none the less a fact that the Great War has proved its correctness on a number of points, and that the opinions advanced by M. Cambon have been supported by other authors, among them Baron Beyens, former Belgian Ambassador in Berlin, in his interesting book "L'Allemagne avant la Guerre."[1] M. Cambon's report, which will always retain the interest attaching to a contemporary document, is essentially as follows:—

From the time of the Morocco conflict up to the present year [1913] an unfriendly feeling towards us Frenchmen has ruled in Germany. The German nation cannot forget that on that occasion we did not retreat, and the decision which we made later with regard to a three years' military service has distinctly increased the general resentment against us. This is especially noticeable now during the Centenary festivities,[2] and the nation is constantly reminded by means of patriotic speeches that France is the hereditary enemy—just as she was a hundred years ago. Nor is it only France which is threatened with war; it is also hanging over the head of Russia. The plan of the German General Staff is, that Germany should try to gain a march on both her chief opponents the instant a crisis arises which is at all likely to develop into a European war. It would thus be necessary for Germany to strike without delay before her opponents have had time to make the necessary preparations.

Stupendous efforts have been made to prepare national feeling for the next war, and in wide and important circles of society they have already established themselves. The nobility and the land-owners—in other words the Junker Party whose family interests and social prestige is essentially

[1] Appeared in the autumn of 1915, and recently translated into English.
[2] This refers to the festivities in 1913, in memory of the rising against Napoleon in 1813.

affected by a war—have made up their minds to
fight. The upper middle class has not the same
direct interest in a war as the Junkers; but from
a social point of view they also look upon war
as a necessity, to check the insubordination of the
labouring class by breaking the power of France,
the home of all revolutionary propaganda. Also
there are those persons who are directly interested
in war, the business men and owners of factories,
makers of cannon and armour-plates, bankers who
speculate in a new age of gold based on the
next war indemnity, the great merchants and those
who are always on the look-out for new markets.
These are joined by the official classes who represent all ranks and all shades of opinion; by the
universities and the higher seats of learning; by
writers on history, philosophy, and politics—all the
typical advocates of their "Kultur," the aim of
which is to compel the rest of humanity into a
special German form of thought.

On the other side stands the great army of
workmen, mechanics, and small tradesmen, all of
them friends of peace, by instinct and interest
alike, but who are not sufficiently organized to
offer the right resistance at the decisive moment.
In the Reichstag there are 110 Social Democrats,
who are all partisans of peace. But at present
they are not in a position to prevent war. Rather
is there reason to believe that they will be swept
along by the general agitation. Therefore the
war must be precipitated—before the Socialists
become so strong that they can stop it once and
for all. The question is now, What attitude did
the Kaiser adopt towards this profound agitation

in the German nation, which a keen-sighted foreigner, with good opportunities for obtaining information, was able to grasp so correctly?

To this it must be answered that a certain phase of development can now be observed in him—a development in the direction of war—evidently a painful development, marked by doubts and inward struggles, but one which inexorably and increasingly took possession of this creature of impulse, who for almost a generation has persuaded his credulous contemporaries into the strange psychological mistake of supposing that he is a strong personality.

At the time of which we now speak official and influential Europe had long recovered from the delusion. King Edward went to his grave in the firm conviction that William II would never give orders to mobilize the German Army. Clemenceau summed him up in the one word *pacifiste*, and the well-known contributor to the *Figaro*, Jean Huret, in 1907 brought home this impression from Potsdam, that "the real nature of the Kaiser is that of a coward."[1] This view, which expressed the feeling in leading military circles in Potsdam and Berlin, aroused Harden's fury, and in a scathing article in the *Zukunft*, under the title of *Wilhelm der Friedliche*,[2] he ridiculed the bare idea that influential people in Germany could entertain such a view, though it was obvious that he himself was inclined to share it, and that, at any rate, he found that there were many plausible grounds for it. But he hinted that

[1] La vraie nature de l'Empereur est celle d'un timide.
[2] William the Peaceful.

if this feeling should show itself so markedly to the Kaiser that he did not dare to maintain the nation's lawful rights, then in that case the nation would have to defend them itself. The words are significant as showing what was thought possible on the Kaiser's part in the way of devotion to peace, in spite of his warlike words. It is known that during the Morocco crisis in the autumn of 1911 the Kaiser was in favour of the amicable solution which had been recommended by the Chancellor in the Reichstag, though it is also an open secret that Germany at that time was financially unprepared for war, and this was a strong additional reason for the cloud passing by. In 1912 his tone became slightly stronger, notably at a banquet given in Berlin to the superior officers of the 3rd Brandenburg Army Corps: " Protected against hostile arrogance and belligerent assaults by a growing Fleet and an Army ready for battle, the peasant may go to his field, the merchant, the manufacturer, and the mechanic to their respective occupations, and the workman may depend upon his well-earned wage."

The remark is of interest, not because it throws any new light upon the actual situation, which, in fact, contained no justification for it, but as an expression of feeling which reflected the forces working at the time within the German nation. It was therefore only a continuation of the same train of thought when immediately after he expressed his firm conviction that the men of Brandenburg would always gather under the banners whenever King and Fatherland should summon them.

BEFORE THE GREAT WAR

But his real change of mind first appeared in 1913—a dangerous year with great temptations for such an impulsive nature as his, even under normal conditions, and more especially at a time when powerful forces in the nation were preparing themselves for a new "War of Liberty" against the hereditary enemy of 1813. The atmosphere became too heated for him. There were too many festivals, too many anniversaries—too many words. He was carried away by the force of circumstances, and at last he was no longer the same man. Cambon confirms this change in his report of November 22, 1913, which contains further particulars of the famous conversation between the Kaiser and the King of the Belgians in the presence of General Moltke some weeks before.[1]

"Hostility against us is becoming more marked," writes the Ambassador, "and the Kaiser has ceased to be a partisan of peace. William II has come to the conclusion that war with France is unavoidable and that it will have to come some day." M. Cambon therefore advised his Government to take into account the new fact that the Emperor was becoming familiar with ideas which formerly repelled him.[2] It appears from Baron Beyens' book that M. Cambon is indebted to him for his knowledge of this conversation, and that he, as well as his colleague, saw clearly that they were facing an entirely new situation.

William II, who, in spite of all his warlike

---

[1] November 6, 1913.
[2] Cf. his conversation reported above with that with Jules Simon, p. 71.

speeches, on many former occasions, had ranged himself on the side of peace, was now in the heart of the war party. Powerless to resist any longer, he floated with the stream down towards the great issue.

"He is not happy," says Beyens, who quotes several remarks from direct conversations with him. "He is serious, almost bitter, and full of reproaches against France. But he retains two illusions which keep him calm and sure of victory in the face of the inevitable.

"He knows from high authority at the Russian Court that the alliance between Russia and France will not stand the strain of a possible Franco-German War, and as for England, he is confident that she will remain neutral."

Thus far we are able to follow him, supported by positive remarks made by himself in conversations with well-known men. Here he stood when the double murder at Serajevo heralded the catastrophe which was to come.

CHAPTER XIX

WILLIAM THE PROBLEM

WHEN the Great War broke out William II had reigned for twenty-six years.

During the whole of that time he had been what we will call in three words *William the Problem*—the great enigma of the time which cast its spell over believers and unbelievers alike, and the grip of which they could not shake off. Shortly before his death in 1892 Ernest Renan regretted that he had to depart this life without knowing the solution of it. In 1891 Eça de Queiroz,[1] one of the finest essayists of Portugal, says he can imagine no other outcome than a European war. Tolstoi lays no small part of the blame for the inordinate dimensions to which the Problem grew upon the uncritical spirit of the times, and benevolent William Stead, comparatively soon came to the conclusion that it was not really very profound. The history of Germany, as we have sketched it in the preceding chapters, tells the same tale on every single page, notwithstanding the official cultivation of fetishes and the " Byzantine " admiration of the people as a whole. At the present time the Problem has lost its interest—not because

[1] Died in 1900.

the unbelievers have facts to their hand which the believers do not yet believe, but because the Problem itself is out of date as a serious factor in the life of our generation—because the stupendous seriousness of the hour has no use for speech-making. We have reached, so to speak, the fifth act of " Hamlet." From the trenches of to-day fragments of wreckage are thrown up to us—parts of the skeleton of European history during the last generation—all contributing to the solution of William the Problem. As we look at these more closely we recognize them, as Hamlet recognized the skull of " poor Yorick " in the famous graveyard scene.

History can afford to be more just towards William II than he has been towards others. It is willing to believe his word when he declares—as he has done, not once but many times—that he ascended the throne with the best intentions and a firm determination to safeguard the peace and secure the welfare of his country. But at the same time it is prepared to maintain, with the hard facts of six and twenty years before it, that the realization of these intentions has been attempted amid such confusion of conflicting ideas and self-contradictions, so much instability and hesitation, both in theory and practice, all supported by such a constant refrain of assurances, " I am on the right course," that one day inevitably it was bound to end in a catastrophe.

William II, by virtue of gifts and qualities which, unfortunately, were so subdivided that they practically produced no effect, very quickly reached the point of being something of a problem. It is in this capacity that he has interested humanity in a deeper sense. People have discussed him and formed theories about him " as there are theories about magnetism, influenza, and the planet Mars." [1] The only difference is that while in the course of years certain definite results had been reached even with regard to the planet Mars, William the Problem was exactly the same enigma in the summer of 1914 as he was in the summer of 1888. People had certainly become more familiar with its various aspects, but there was no means of establishing any general rule. His speeches, which, even in 1902, amounted, according to a German computation, to " well over four hundred," and can now probably be estimated at one thousand at the least, help us very little. Neither in themselves nor with regard to the Problem can they be said to enrich mankind either morally or spiritually. No one after reading them will carry away any impression of that modesty of character which is the most unmistakable sign of a great soul. No one will learn from them the difficult art of self-criticism or enlarge his political wisdom with a single idea or enrich his fancy with a single image. They are as barren as a barrack square, full of words and phrases in full uniform marching up in review order. They flash and crackle with summer lightning and unexpected explosions, but they kindle no real fire, because behind them there is neither a mighty spirit nor a mighty heart. It is only when he speaks of the sea that now and then a trace of genuine feeling comes into them ; but it is not long before the voice of

[1] Quotation from da Queiroz.

command breaks in and spoils everything. As a preacher, he has an Old Testament wealth of expression which is not without a temporary effect, even on the mind of a reader. But the oratorical structure is not strong enough either in thought or feeling to carry such a load, and the consequence is that it all collapses in a turmoil of words. The reason for this is manifest to every one who has attempted to form a personal opinion on the Problem. Its purpose in the world—as far as can yet be discerned—is to serve as a typical contradiction, loaded with conceptions and theories which humanity has long since outgrown, and within the narrow circle of which all living things die. Thus there is all the more room left for it. It fills the horizon, not in virtue of its originality but because of its unusualness, and instead of imprinting itself on the age the Problem itself varies according to the shifting circumstances of the hour. Here we touch on a central point in William II, his moral and spiritual incompleteness—or, in other words, just those qualities which have made him a problem. In him as in Hamlet there are elements of various men, and it is chance that determines which of them predominates. Events come and go. One after another situations arise which would seem to compel a change. Now we must surely see something ! But that which Nora [1] calls " the marvellous " may keep us waiting from year to year. Even the Great War has not given us the solution of the Problem.

What is the reason of this?

Because his capacity for development has never

[1] " The Doll's House," by Ibsen.

WILLIAM THE PROBLEM

extended beyond the range of the remarkable. But on this lower plane of human perfection it can be freely admitted that he has performed the incredible. On the strength of a versatility in powers and interests which excludes everything that can be called originality or profundity, he has come to be regarded as an authority on subjects upon which other men have laboured all their lives and yet freely admit that they have not mastered them. With a beaming assurance which is fostered as much by his inborn childishness as by his exalted position he has misinterpreted in the most unique fashion the classic phrase " Nothing that is human is alien to me." The beautiful attitude of mind which conceived the thought has been changed in him to a matter-of-fact notion. Through his striking journalistic gifts, coupled with bodily endurance far above the ordinary, he has found opportunity for expressing his views on all the great questions of the time and many of the lesser ones—all with an easy unaffectedness which simply makes other people feel absolutely ashamed of themselves.

Socialism? " Leave Socialism to me. I will soon dispose of that."

Woman's purpose in the world? " *Kirche, Küche, Kinder*." [1] What a pity that Stuart Mill did not live to hear this marvellous formula in three K's, as simple as the egg of Columbus.

The great aim of religion? " To make good soldiers, of course. There is no good soldier who is not a good Christian."

The eight greatest men who have ever lived?

[1] Church, kitchen, children.

"Hammurabi,[1] Abraham, Moses, Homer, Luther, Shakespeare, Goethe, and the Emperor William the Great."

Examples could be multiplied. To every question he has an answer ready, partly because he himself is an adept in the art of questioning, and he delivers his answers to the stupefaction of the public. The consequence is that for years he has made a disproportionate impression on his fellow-men, especially those who have come into direct contact with him, and also on the millions and millions who have only had the opportunity of watching him from the gallery. Admiration has spread from the nearest to the farthest, encouraged by the worst and the most corrupt examples. It has degraded literature, the Press, the pulpit, and public education in a way which has no parallel in our time, and has created a particular kind of eloquence, loud-voiced and undiscerning, armed with catchwords from the Imperial arsenal. What has been thus accomplished in Germany, especially in that "William II." literature, with its constant tendency to increase, is calculated to make even an unprejudiced German feel ill at ease. "These books and pamphlets," says Count Reventlow in his well-known book *Kaiser Wilhelm II und die Byzantiner*, exhibit all shades of admiration from the most fulsome and unblushing praise to the most refined methods of what in mathematics is called the indirect proof." He points out how this spiritual infection breeds and spreads, and there is abundant evidence that he does not stand alone

---

[1] A Babylonian king, born 2267, died 2213 B.C.

in his observations. The mischief goes beyond the frontier, and one fine day there springs up somewhere abroad a brilliant toadstool which is immediately imported and exhibited as a flower for the inspection and admiration of the nation. One example will illustrate the fact. Some years ago a little Dutch provincial paper contained the following tribute to the Kaiser, which immediately made the round of the official German Press as representing opinion abroad :—

"He is endowed with mental gifts which exceed those of all prominent figures of our age. From the Great Elector he has inherited his intrepidity and his inflexibility ; from Frederick I his love of show and pageantry ; from Frederick William I his strong feelings of duty and responsibility ; from Frederick II his high wisdom, his keen diplomatic intelligence, his love of art and beauty. Through ceaseless labour he has formed an opinion of his own on German history, on the development of German strength and German intellect, on German art and literature. He is familiar with the latest problems in natural science ; he understands economic conditions throughout the world ; he is fully experienced in all branches of military service and in the affairs of the Navy. He is a connoisseur in music and the plastic arts, and besides all this he has found time for hunting and sport. Everything that he undertakes bears the stamp of thoroughness and permanency. What he knows, he knows completely. Every word which is spoken by a man of such proportions deserves to be heard."

This quotation gives us in a word the secret

of William the Problem which for years has been impregnating the minds of this generation with the most supreme contempt, not only for facts but also for human intelligence. Unfettered spirits among the great civilized nations—not least in Germany—have attempted, time after time, to reduce the problem to its proper dimensions, which is equal to saying that they would take it out of the field of discussion. But that unlucky tendency to the cult of the individual which is so deeply rooted in the German nation, together with the robust tenacity they exhibit when it is a question of gaining admittance for something of their own to the notice of strangers, has naturally made the efforts of independent characters quite fruitless. It has flattered the self-esteem of the Germans to know that their Kaiser was the most discussed of the world's potentates. They have advertised him from one country to another as they have advertised their motors, their dyestuffs, and their toys, without perceiving that the position was not exactly the same. *Unser Kaiser* was unique. He could repeat the names of all the Assyrian kings; he knew everything about Germany, both in ancient and modern times; he could draw and compose, conduct an orchestra, deliver sermons and lectures, instruct actors, and undertake demonstrations in the art of cookery. In a word, he had most of the attributes which have never been considered necessary for the head of a State, and he had not the one great gift of leading his people safely and steadily through times of transition. But there were comparatively few who realized this. By indulging freely in all these remarkable tastes, by cultivating the national love of advertisement instead of restraining it, by parading his uniforms and his colours over a whole continent, and raising altars to deceased Hohenzollerns from the North Cape to Corfu, he gradually became to the average German something like a conqueror's banner, which acted upon the man in the street as the crescent acted on the Turks in the days of the Caliphate.

> In diesem Bau giebst du der Welt ein Zeichen!
> Dein Wollen steigt anf flügelstarker Spur.
> Am Schwert die Faust, ein Schildherr ohne Gleichen
> Bist du ein Mehrer schaffender Kultur.[1]

This verse was undoubtedly "made in Germany," or to put it more exactly, it was evolved quite spontaneously under the spiked helmet of a poetic major, who did nothing more or less than transform one of the many Imperial speeches into verse. But the meaning is clear enough.

Cave! Adsum! Thus Prince William threatened Bismarck in the middle of the 'eighties. He had ruled through the 'nineties in accordance with that threat, and now on the threshold of the twentieth century the same warning sounded like an echo of the *Weltpolitik*, with its head strong ambition. Bismarck had smiled at "the formidableness of youth," and official Europe had seen so many extraordinary results of the Imperial zigzag policy that it had gradually come to look upon him as a harmless *pacifiste* who had not

[1] From the "Prologue" on the Inauguration Day of the Reichs-Limes Museum.

conquered a bad habit of clanking his sword and spurs in a somewhat noisy manner. The German Navy Act with its extensive programme, the agitation with regard to the Fleet, and the new colonial policy as we have indicated them in their main features, the intensified displeasure of the nation under the strain of the disappointments it has suffered, not so much as a result of the action of others as because of the Kaiser's own words—all these became elements in favour of William II in his official capacity as representative of the German nation, and bore witness to an increasing power which foreign States were bound to consider in their political calculations. It was therefore by no accident that the *Entente* efforts which brought France and England together in 1904, and which in 1907 welded in Russia as a link in the same chain, took their permanent shape during the ten years immediately following the first great Navy Act. Never had William II's policy been more ostentatious than during these years. Involuntarily the Great Powers yielded step by step. One dramatic victory after another was won. There was the affair of Tangiers, with its humiliation for France. There was the "shining armour" episode, with its equally undoubted humiliation for Russia. There was the neutralization of the second Hague Conference—an act of vital importance to the armament policy, without which it could not go or undisturbed. But in the midst of all this, international indignation grew stronger and stronger without the majority of the German nation seeming to notice it. The "Morocco" summer of 1911 threw a strong ray of light on the dangerous policy which was practised in virtue of William the Problem. But instead of sweeping in front of its own door—a task which, for obvious reasons, does not appeal to a nation which is constantly busy outside the doors of others—the nation did not learn anything from what had happened. Europe must be made to understand that she was on the brink of a great issue, and in order that no one should be in doubt as to its meaning General von Bernhardi dismounted from his charger and wrote *Deutschland und der nächste Krieg*.[1]

Side by side with all this there was still an interchange of empty phrases and high-flown words, not only between the Kaiser and his " dynastic guests," but also between representatives of the various nations—the reciprocal visit of the German and British journalists in 1907 being one of the most illustrative examples. But these exceptions only serve to emphasize the rule. They were carried out in so conspicuous a manner as to confirm an impression of previous arrangement. People could not get rid of the disastrous " Beware ! I am at hand ! " In this way the Kaiser gradually grew to be among his own people something almost supernatural. We have mentioned the natural explanations of the phenomenon —the thoughtlessness and folly of the masses, the shamelessness of the Byzantine Press, the degradation of literature, of public worship, and of public education in the service of the Hohenzollern cult. But there is also another fact of importance which

[1] "Germany and the Next War."

has to be taken into account—a mental connection which forms a link between William II and the German nation and which is its outward, if not exactly its inward, strength to-day. William II did not come headlong in among the German people as, for example, Napoleon did among the French—almost a foreigner, but one who knew how to play on every chord in them with the facility of a virtuoso. On the contrary, he had grown organically out of it, and he shared its good and bad qualities—its tenacity, its energy, its importunate benevolence, its set phrases, and its official conception of life. There is nothing in him of that Germany which in *Sturm und Drang* [1] had raised new ideals in the development of the generations and to which the world will remain indebted for all time, in spite of the ruined Library of Louvain and the battered Cathedral of Rheims. It is sufficient to mention in this connection that on Schiller's Day in 1905—amid the celebrations of that important anniversary, which was something of an international event—he found no greater or more worthy task than that of holding a military review in Strassburg. On the other hand, he is a modern Berlin citizen intensified, and he draws the majority after him through the labyrinth of his ideas—ideas more startling than really original—because the whole thing goes at such lightning speed and with such a constantly changing programme. *Er ist ein moderner Mensch* [2] was the judgment passed upon him by a conspicuous member of the Reichstag during a sitting some years ago. The expression is excel-

---

[1] Storm and stress.   [2] He is a modern man.

WILLIAM THE PROBLEM

lent—if the word "modern" be taken in its least exalted meaning. It is in truth this which makes William II the typical German he is, and also an ordinary citizen of the world. He represents the spirit of the age—its self-advertisement, its smartness, its competitive eagerness, and, not least, its untiring energy in making and breaking records. He is at once the nation's referee, who follows it all the world over, stop-watch in hand, and announces the results, and the Imperial Champion who has long held the world's record for unexpectedness and who has already, in the first lap, easily spurted past half a score of his royal "cousins."

But even all this is not enough to make him a problem.

The enigmatical—or to speak less ceremoniously —the interesting side of him first shows at the moment when all this modern intensity combines with a conception of authority which men left behind them centuries ago, and which has no real meaning for a modern man.

The point of departure can be expressed in the famous words, "We Hohenzollerns owe our position to God alone, and before God alone are we responsible for the duties it involves"; and the proof can be shown in the no less characteristic words, "Soldiers and armies, not parliamentary majorities and resolutions, have welded the German Empire together."

Upon these quite primitive theories, of which the first is an empty assertion and the second only half a truth, the whole of that Imperial absolutism was built which William II was never tired of proclaiming. German writers who have wished to exclude the idea of vanity as something foreign to his nature have given themselves much trouble to explain that it was not in the least for his own sake that he desired all these peacock feathers of power which he had opened out in the course of years into such a magnificent fan. It is from respect to that kingship by the grace of God to which he was born, and the idea of which he regards it as his exalted mission to keep alive among the children of men. Therefore he assumes all burdens, great and small alike, with a conscientious thoroughness that knows no equal, and still finds time to strike a blow for his " cousins," whose ideas as to their position are liable to be blunted in their somewhat over-parliamentary surroundings. Practically speaking, this explanation of his attitude makes little difference. As " the last feudal lord " who has received his crown direct from God, and who one day will be called to account as to how he has used his privilege, the vocation of King and Emperor has a significance for him which would crush him utterly if he did not feel that he lived day by day in spiritual intercourse with the King of Kings—*unser alter deutscher Gott*.[1] He laboured to make the nation see things in the same light, and with his strange weakness for reckoning as facts things which are only fanciful aspirations he saw the German nation filled with the spirit of monarchy—so much so as to be sufficient, not only for himself but to serve as a reserve supply at the disposition of others. His " dynastic guests " grew physically and spiritually

[1] Our old German God.

to overwhelming dimensions, and on behalf of his people he proclaimed to them what Germany's feelings were. On one occasion, several days after the departure of the present Tsar—an unassuming, slightly built man—the Kaiser protested that they all still felt " the influence of that heroic figure of knightly romance"; and towards the King of Spain, some years later, he expressed his firm conviction that " the German nation daily unites in prayer " on that young ruler's behalf.

By magnifying the idea of monarchy to a superhuman extent, looking on himself as the high priest of this cult at home and abroad, and by labouring at it unceasingly, by word and deed he needed only to take one step to arrive at, not only a personal but even a directly familiar relation with the God he so constantly invoked. Since the days of Moses the world has not seen such an intimacy between the Creator and one of His creatures, and, like his great prototype, he proclaims loudly and frequently, so that no one can be in doubt or say that he has not heard it, that between God and himself in his capacity of King and Emperor—" the gracious God and I "—there is a temporal and spiritual alliance which makes him strong, and which through him flows rich with blessings to his people and bears a message to all the rest of humanity. Arm in arm with " our Ally from Rossbach and Deannewitz " under the eye of Kaiser William the Great and his paladins who look down from their heaven, he has gone about the world in an exuberance of confidence —*Optimist durch und durch*,[1] as he said of

[1] Optimistic through and through.

himself—" specially protected " on his road towards " glorious days."

And by degrees not only he but also the German nation are supposed to occupy a peculiar position with higher, more exalted, duties than those of others.

"Russians, Frenchmen, Englishmen—whoever they may be—all struggle for civilization. We Germans also think of something higher—namely, our religion."[1]

The remark is typical and stands in close connection with the even more characteristic speech which we have already quoted.

"We are the salt of the earth." Here we have the missionary idea clearly formulated, the programme decided, and the road marked out: "Go forth, ye Germans, and conquer the world. We are the first in science, mechanics, and art, and in those directions where we still lack something we are going to work ourselves up into the first rank. Look at the statistics. We pass one opponent after another, beat our own records and other people's, and constantly establish new standards. *Gott mit uns!*"

By degrees the nation was gradually hypnotized —a condition easily reached by the German temperament, childish and unreflecting, devoid of political instinct, with a tendency to mysticism and an almost boundless faith in authority. William the Problem, a thing which originally only concerned Germany, grew into the problem of *Deutschtum*—a new conception of vastly greater

[1] From the speech made in Wilhelmshaven to the first expeditionary force to China.

dimensions which concerns the whole outside world. Scientifically it had already become something of a philosophical system, even before the end of the century,[1] and by degrees evolved its own peculiar morality with two main divisions: the first including all that is permitted to the Germans, the second all that is forbidden to the rest of the world—which in practice comes to the same thing.

The Kaiser and Harden—*les extrêmes se touchent*—share the same fundamental view, the only difference being that Harden ventures to trace the inevitable consequence of that Imperial remark about *civis Romanus*—namely, that " we Germans are not to be judged by other Europeans."

In these words, which embody the whole psychology of the War, as far as Germany is concerned, there is no longer any question about the subjective will, either in the Kaiser or in the bulk of his countrymen. What comes into operation is a complete system—psychic, political, social, and economical forces combined—all that in the course of years has made possible the development of a type like William II, and given it such an ominous influence tending more than others towards the catastrophe which some few far-sighted mortals prophesied nearly a generation ago.

We fully agree with those who maintain—even in England—that William II never consciously willed the war; but it is equally certain that he has been unconsciously working up to it ever since his first threats on the eighth anniversary of Mars

[1] Cf. Professor Gallwitz's article "Vom deutschen Gott" in *Preussische Jahrbucher*, 1899.

la Tours.[1] The German people share his guilt
indirectly—because they did not protest against
the Imperial declamations, because for twenty-six
years they allowed him to trifle with war and
with the thoughts of war, in the midst of a perfect
torrent of assurances of peace, so that by degrees
a confusion was established between dreams and
realities, between theory and fact. We have seen
how from time to time the nation has reacted—
above all, in 1908—and that it was clear to a
far greater part of it than one would think possible
that things were taking place which might one
day place Germany face to face with a situation
of the most amazing consequence. But the system
was too powerful and the nation's powers of
" going from political comprehension to practical
action" too weak for this to make much difference.[2] Therefore it came about that William II,
through the strong and weak points in his people,
as well as through those in himself, was necessarily
a contradiction in his day. The man who introduced himself as something of an unrecognized
genius, and who tried to prove his contention by
giving the world the most astounding surprises,
ended by representing himself and his people as
innocent creatures, hemmed in by a ring of
enemies. Therefore history, for which William II
has never been more than a problem for men
to sharpen their wits upon in hours of ease, has
no use for him in the greatest, most stupendous
crisis in the life of the German nation. He who
in the days of peace always had something to say

[1] Cf. with p. 33.
[2] From Prince Bülow's book " Imperial Germany."

has become remarkably taciturn in this time of war. Also the little that he does say has changed its character. He has nothing left to point at—not one illusion which can serve as a programme at the moment. He only has excuses—a substitute he did not know before—and in face of the horror of the moment there is nothing left of the pride of " the Roman citizen "; " In compulsory self-defence, with clear conscience and clean hands. . . ."[1]

But history, which has no use for protestations like these in such a moment, follows him discreetly to his motor-car and shuts the door. How long he will remain in that car—speeding furiously between two fronts—the future alone can show. He himself seems to think that there is plenty of time. Last autumn he worked out some elaborate regulations for new uniforms to be worn in peace-time, with a wealth of directions about materials and colours, gaiters and boots, epaulettes and bandoliers, cords and tassels, and all the rest of the accoutrements.[2]

" What a comedy ! But it is nothing more ! "

Nevertheless—and here William the Man and William the Problem meet in that higher, unalterable unity which must be added to complete the picture—what we have called the " Prologue " is followed by its natural " Epilogue ": " For, gentlemen, I am a soldier."

Germany's sacrifices are greater, her wounds

[1] From the speech from the throne at the opening of the Reichstag on August 4, 1914.
[2] Published in the *Armee Verordnungsblatt* and subsequently in the German daily press in the beginning of October, 1915.

more terrible, than at any previous moment in her history; it is the tragedy of Fate for the nation which allowed itself to be led unresistingly towards " glorious days."

But the Kaiser does not forget his people. They have their reward in the promise of new uniforms.

LITERATURE CONCERNING WILLIAM II

ACCORDING to Karl Georg's well-known "Schlagwortkatalog" for 1910 over four hundred books and pamphlets concerning William II have been published in the last twenty-two years. Since then the number has considerably increased on account of his twenty-five years' jubilee and the centenary jubilee of German liberation, which coincided in 1913.

It stands to reason that such an enormous production excludes the possibility of genuine intimate knowledge or criticism, and the titles themselves show that quite a disproportionate number of these books and pamphlets have made it their first and most important object to glorify rather than to describe. They contain, therefore, very little real historical matter. Of the more important German works on William II and his times we may name :—

WILHELM II. die Reden Kaiser Wilhelms II (Reclams Universal Bibliothek. 4th vol., Nos. 3658-60, 4548-50, 4903-5, 5561-2 respectively). The Imperial speeches up to the end of 1912.

A. OSKAR KLAUSSMANN. Kaiserreden (1888-1902). Speeches letters, rescripts, and telegrams, arranged to give a *Charakterbild* of the Kaiser (1902).

E. SCHRÖDER. Zwanzig Jahre Regierungszeit : ein Tagebuch Kaiser Wilhelms II (June 15, 1888, to June 15, 1908). Nach Hof und andere Berichten (1908).

G. HINTZPETER. Kaiser Wilhelm II : ein Skizze nach der Natur gezeichnet (1888).

OTTO MITTELSTÄDT. Vor der Fluth ; sechs Briefe zur Politik der deutschen Gegenwart (1898).

PAUL LIMAN. Der Kaiser : Versuch einer Charakteristik Kaiser Wilhelms II 1889-1909. (3rd Edition 1911.)

F. von Bernhardi. Deutschland und der nächste Krieg (1911).
Karl Lamprecht. Der Kaiser: Versuch einer Charakteristik (1913).
Graf E. Reventlow. Kaiser Wilhelm und die Byzantiner (1906); Deutschlands auswärtige Politik 1888–1913 (1913).
Felix Rachfal. Kaiser und Reich 1888–1913 (1913).
Deutschland unter Kaiser Wilhelm II (I–III). Containing contributions by a number of excellent authorities, among them being Prince Bülow. (Cf. page 53.) 1911.
Fürst Chlodwig zu Hohenlohe Schillingsfürst. Denkwürdigkelten i.–ii. (1907), published by Friedrich Curtius.
Maximilian Harden. Köpfe i.–iii. (1910–13).

The principal magazines in Germany, England, and France (1888–1913) contain an abundance of information with respect to William II's personality and the most important events of his reign concerning international policy before the Great War. Besides these, there are, published at the same period, numberless monographs on the Kaiser in French and English, and also many works on his times. The Great War has contributed to the increase of this literature, especially in England, and new works are constantly appearing.

From the French point of view "The French Yellow Book" and Baron Beyen's "l'Allemagne avant la Guerre" (mentioned page 237) are important immediate contributions to explain the psychology of the Kaiser and the general feeling in Germany immediately before the Great War.

INDEX

Aachen, speech of William II at, 199-200
Abdul Hamid, 45, 143-4
Aehrenthal, Count, 231
Agadir incident, the, 235-6, 240, 252-3
Albrecht, Duke of Prussia, 84
Aldershot, 43
Alexander III of Russia, 44, 59
Alexandra, Queen, 229
Algeciras, 230
Alsace-Lorraine, visit of Wiliiam II to, 44; question of, 184
America Cup, the, 127
Arbitration Between Nations, British and Foreign Association for, 92
Army, the, proclamation of William II to, 30; Army Act, 1893, 101; speech of William II at Potsdam, 1898, 138; the rescript of 1890, 151-3; a question of uniform, 153-4; manœuvres, 154-5
Arthur, Port, fall of, 206
Atlantic record, the, 127
Augusta, Empress, 44-5
Augusta Victoria, Kaiserin, 16, 18
Austria, relations with Napoleon III, 1-2; William II's alliance with, 32, 43; treaty with Germany, 1879, 58-9; effect of the Reassurance Treaty on, 87 annexation of Bosnia, 231

Baden, 44, 127
Baden, Grand Duke of, 12-13; and Swiss neutrality, 50-1; on Bismarck's fall, 54

Bagdad Railway, the, 143
Balkan Peninsula, situation in the, 58, 236; policy of William II, 45
Bassermann on the Breslau speech, 212-13
Bavaria, visit of torpedo flotilla, 127
Berchtesgaden, 219
Berlepsch, Herr von, 61
Berlin, excitement on birth of William II, 3; the Tiergarten Railway Station, 43; Moltke's memorial in the Königsplatz, 211
Berlin City Council, William II and the, 38-9
Berlin Congress, treatment of Russia, 58
Berlin Treaty, 1878, terms, 231
Berliner Tageblatt, articles *cited*, 29-30
Bernhardi, General von, book of, 253
Beyens, Baron, *L'Allemagne avant la Guerre*, 236-8, 241-2
Bieberstein, Marschall von, the Kruger telegram, 116-17
Bielefeld, 149
Bismarck, "Bill," 46
Bismarck, Count Herbert, 46, 98-100
Bismarck, Frau Johanna, 81
Bismarck, Prince, relations with William II, 1, 19-20, 21-3, 40-1, 63, 169, 222, 251; Frederick III and, 24-7; Russian policy, 32, 53, 58-9, 68; visit from the Kaiser, 34-5; royal telegrams from Athens, 45-6; intrigues

against, 46-52; causes of his fall, 53-66; speech in the Reichstag, 1889, *cited*, 57; relations with Austria, 58-9; policy towards England, 68; relations with Caprivi, 81; illness 1893, 101-2; death, 145; remarks of, *quoted*, 148; description of Count Waldersee, 163; saying of, regarding Kiao-Chao, 189

Bleichröder, Herr, 63

Blücher, 201

Bohemia, visit to, 222

Bon, Signor Saint, 37

Bonn, University of, 10-11

"Borusser Corps," the, 11, 233

Bosnia, 231

Boxer riots in China, 1900, 157-66

Brandenburg Army Corps, 3rd, speech of William II to, 240

Bremen, monument to William I, 73-6; visit in 1901, 174-7; speech of William II at, 207-8

Bremen Chamber of Commerce, report of 1901, 129

Bremenhafen, speech of William II at, 1900, 159-60

Breslau, 35, 150; speech of William II at, 212

Bronsart, 140

Bülow, Prince, *Deutsche Politik cited*, 69; reply to the Chinese Emperor, 161; appointed Chancellor, 180-2; on the American visit of Prince Henry, 193; foreign policy, 208-9; his title, 211; and the Imperial interview, 219-21, 225-6; retirement, 233-4

Cabinet Order of 1852, 62-3; Bismarck's protest, 64

Cambon, M. Jules, the "Yellow Book," 236; on William II, 241

Cambridge, Duke of, 43

Capitol, the, Rome, 36

Caprivi, General von, successor to Bismarck, 53, 61, 79, 81, 87, 96, 100-1, 224; letter of, regarding the Bismarck wedding, 98-99; dismissal, 103-5; Colonial Office established, 120-1; naval policy, 123; and the Revolt Act, 132; foreign policy, 204

Castellamare, 36

Century Magazine, report of the Imperial interview, 226

Chance, games of, denounced by the Kaiser, 152

Chat Noir, Berlin, 223

China, Boxer riots, 1900, 157-66; Russia's policy towards, 203-4

Chino-Japanese War, results, 114-15

Chirol, Sir Valentine, 185

Christian Socialists, 48

Christiania, 85

Chun, Prince, 165

Clemenceau, M., 239

Cologne, 127

Constantine, King, 44

Constantinople, 45, 143

Contemporary Reiew, 1892, *quoted*, 94

Copenhagen, 34

Corfu, 45

Cowes Regatta, 1895, 114

Crispi, 37

Daily Telegraph, publication of the personal interview, 215-16, 220-7

Damascus, 144

Dannewitz, 257

Dardanelles, 45

Darmstadt, 84

Delagoa Bay, 117

Delbrück, Professor, 150

Delcassé, M., 146; resignation, 210-11

INDEX

der neue Herr, 80
Dernburg, Herr, on Eulenburg, 104–5
Deutsche Rundschau, publication of the "Diaries," 38
Deutschland über Alles, 70
Dewey, Admiral, 189
Die Flotte, 125
Die Grenzboten, 129
Die Post, on the Imperial interview, *quoted*, 219
Donaueschingen, 223
Dover, 43
Dreadnought, the, visit of William II, 45–6
Dresden, battle of, 35
Dresden, Bismarck at, 100
Dreyfus case, the, 146
Dryander, Rev., 201 *n*.

Edison, 44
Education, public school in Germany, 7–9
Edward VII (as Prince of Wales) in Berlin, 71–2; visit in 1909, 229; his opinion of William II, 239
Elementary School Act, 101
Elizabeth, Empress of Austria, 84
Emanuel, Victor, 37
England, visit of the Kaiser, 1889, 42; policy of Bismarck towards, 68; subsequent visits, 85, 91–4, 110–18; William II and, 87–8; appointment of Count Waldersee, 164; German feeling regarding, 182–6; the alliance with Japan, 183–4, 189; proposal to reduce armaments, 233; commercial treaty with Germany, 230; William's hope of her neutrality, 242
Entente, the, 252
Essen, 150; William II at, 85
Eulenburg, Count, influence on William II, 79; defeat of Caprivi, 104–5

Fashoda incident, the, 147
Figaro, the, 239
First Foot Guards, part played by the, 11–12
First Navy Act, 121–8
First Prussian Guards, uniform changes, 153
France, William II and, 33–4, 146; Hohenlohe and, 135
Francis-Ferdinand, Archduke, 222–3
Francis-Joseph, 43
Franco-British Morocco Agreement of 1904, 208–11
Franco-German War, effects, 12–13, 47, 196
Franco-Russian Alliance, 59, 91, 93
Frankfort-on-the-Main, 223
Frankfurter Zeitung, the, on German foreign policy, 202–3
Frederick I, 234
Frederick III, on war, *quoted*, 17; succession, 22–3; proclamation and aims, 24–7; "Diaries of the Emperor Frederick," 38–40
Frederick the Great, 83–4; bronze statue of, sent to America, 193
Frederick, Empress, birth of William II, 2–5; and her son, 17; Memoirs, 26–7
Frederick-Charles, Prince, statue to, 33–4
Frederick-William I, 234
Frederick-William III, 229
Frederick-William IV, 1, 83
Frederick-William of Brandenburg, 15–16, 83 *n*.; jubilee of, 168
Freiligrath, poet, 109
Friedrichsruhe, 34, 57, 70, 100, 102
Fürstenberg, Prince, 11, 223, 224

INDEX

Gazette, the, letter of Princess Victoria to, 4–5
Geffcken, Dr. Robert, 38
George V. at the International Labour Congress, 71 ; journey as Prince of Wales, 186
German Confederation, and the Naval movement, 127
Germersheim, 127
Gladstone, W. E., and Abdul Hamid, 143
Goethe, *quoted*, 10, 18, 67, 72, 125, 171, 214
Golden Bull, the, *quoted*, 63
Gossler, Herr von, 165–6
Gravelotte, 12
" Great Knife (The)," 157–8
Greece, 44–5
Guildhall, London, 92–4

Hague Conference, the first, 187 ; the second, 252
Hamburg, 128 ; opening of harbour, 35
HamburgerNachrichten, the, *cited*, 59
Hammerstein, 47–8
Hankow, 114
Hanover, visits to, 44 ; the Waterloo column, 147 ; speech of William II, 201
Harden, Maximilian, on William II, 177 ; on the Imperial interview, 219 ; article in the *Zukunft*, 239 ; opinions of, 259
Heine, 221
Heligoland Agreement, 1890, 88–90
Helmholtz, 18
Henry, Prince, 123 ; mission to China, 141–2 ; visit to America, 190–9, 203
Herbette, M., 97
Hertha, the, 124 *n.*
Herzegovina, 231

Hessen, 127
Hintzpeter, Dr., *quoted*, 5–6, 11, 21, 232
Hohenlohe, Prince, " Memoirs "of, *quoted*, 16, 47, 50–1, 53–4, 70–1, 89, 102, 184 ; Chancellorship, 132–4, 178–80
Hohenzollern, the, speech of William II on, 1900, 161–2
Holleben, von, recall, 202
Hollman, Admiral, letter from William II, 201
Hollweg, Chancellor Bethmann, at Bonn, 11 ; and the proposed reduction of armaments, 233–4
Holstein, Baron von, 185
Holtzendorff, Admiral von, 223–4
Hoyos, Margarethe, 98
Humbert, King, visit of William II to, 36
Huret, Jean, opinion of the Kaiser, 239

Ibsen, " The Doll's House," *quoted*, 246
Imperial Shipbuilding League, 111–12
International Labour Conference, 1890, 60–3, 71–3
Italy, William II and, 32 ; the break up of the Triple Alliance, 189

Jagow, von, 11
Jameson, Dr., raid of, 115–19
Japan, Treaty of Shimoniseki, 114–15 ; the war with Russia, 155–6 ; alliance with England, 183–4, 189 ; Russian policy towards, 203 ; opposed to Germany in 1914, 205 ; attitude of William II towards, 227
Jerusalem, " Church of the Redeemer " in, 143–4
Journalists, British, and German reciprocal visits, 253

INDEX

Juan Shi Kai, 158 n.
Jubilee year, the, 106–19

Kaiser Alexander Regiment, speech to the, 176–7
Kaiser Karl der Grosse, 128
Kaiser Wilhelm der Grosse, 128
Kassel, the gymnasium, 7–9
Ketteler, Freiherr von, murder of, 158–65
Kiau-Chau, 121, 140–1, 158, 189
Kiel, 32, 128, 223–4
Kissingen, Bismarck at, 100–2
Kitchener, Lord, 147
Knackfuss, Prof., painting of, 159–60, 204
Koester, Admiral von, 124
Kölnische Zeitung, 39
Königsberg, 149; speech at, 1910, 234–5
Kopenick incident, the, 214
Kreuzzeitung, the, articles *quoted*, 47, 105
Kronstadt, 91
Kruger telegram, the, 115–19, 147–8
Krupp's, 85
"Kultur," 238
Kupfergraben, 176

Labour Congress, International, 60–3, 71–3
Lauenburg, Duke of, title conferred on Bismarck, 65
Leipzig, law courts, 35
Leo XIII, visit of William II to, 36
Lessing, *Minna von Barnhelm*, 80
Lichterfeld, 85
Lippe-Detmold, Prince, 35
Lithuania, 91
Loewenfeld, General von, 224
London, excitement on birth of William II, 3; visit of the Kaiser, 1891, 92–4
Louisa, Queen, 235
Louvain, 254

Luther, 84
Lucanus, Herr von, 105, 180–1

Macedonia, 204
Malplaquet, 43, 229
Malta, 45–6
Manchuria, 205
Maracaibo, 203
Mars-la-Tours, 33–4, 259–60
Maurenbrecher, Prof., 20
Meline, M., 146
Memel, 91
Meteor, launch of the, 189–99
Mill, Stuart, 247
Mittelstädt, Otto, 69
Moltke, Count von, 48, 72–3, 84, 211–12, 241
Mommsen, Prof., 150–1
Monroe Doctrine, the, 183, 202
Morocco, Franco-British agreement, 1904, 208–11; Algeciras, 230; the Agadir, 235–6, 240, 252–3
Munich, 35; Bismarck at, 100
Murat, Joachim, 36

Naples, visit of William II, 36–7
Napoleon III, relations with Austria, 1–2; the German victories, 12; the rising against, 237
Narva, 91
Navy, the, proclamation of William II, 30; the Kaiser a British admiral, 42–5; his interest in 109–13; the First Navy Act, 121–8; the Naval Department, 123–4; the Chinese expedition, 173; speech of Hohenlohe on the Navy Bill, 179; Acts, 1906–13, 185–6; the speech at Bremen, 207–8; new saluting regulations at Kiel, 223–4; England's proposal to reduce armaments, 233
Navy League, the, 123–8

Nelson, German admiration for, 111
New York Times, 226
New York World, publication of the Imperial interview, 227
Nicholas II, peace manifesto, 1898, 187; William II and, 204; visit to Germany, 257
Nogi, General, 206
Norddeutsche Allgemeine Zeitung, 33, 167; report of the Imperial interview, 218-19
Norderney, 219-20
North German Lloyd line, the, 73
Norway, visits to, 42

Oeynhausen, 149
Ohnet, Georges, 72, 136
Old Age and Disablement Insurance Bill, 51-2
Omdurman, 147
Oscar, King, 85
Otto III, 194

Palestine, visit of William II to, 142-4
Panther, the, at Agadir, 235-6
Pape, General, 84
Parthenon, the, 45
Peking, Boxer rising, 157-66
Pemba, 88
"Penance Mission" from China, 165
Pericles, 45
Peterhof, 33
Petropaulovsk, loss of the, 205
Philippine War, the, 1898, 189
"Poem to Ægir," 104
Poland, Russian troops in, 205
Portugal, commercial treaty with Germany, 230
Portuguese in Africa, 117
Potsdam, 138
Preussische Jahrbucher, the, 150
Prison Act, the, 149

Prussian Guard, the, William's appeal to, 178
Prussian War Office centenary, 229
Prussians, the, proclamation of the Emperor Frederick to, 24-5; proclamation of William II, 30-1
Public School education, William II on, 7-9

Queich River, 127
Queiroz, Eca da, *quoted*, 243, 245
Quirinal, the, 36

Reassurance Treaty, the, 58-9, 87
"Red Fist (The)," 157-8
Reichsanzeiger, the, 99; on the Imperial interview, 225
Reichs-Limes-Museum, dedication, 166-8, 180 *n.*, 251
Reichstag, the, speeches of the Kaiser, 31-2, 212, 261
Reims, 254
Religion, William II and, 247-8
Renan, Ernest, 243
Reventlow, Count, book of, *quoted* 182, 248; policy, 209
"Revolt Act," the, 103-4, 131, 149
Rhodes, Cecil, 103
Richter, Eugen, 46
Roberts, Lord, 148, 217
Rome, visit of William II, 35-6; Bülow's villa at, 220
Rominten, 219, 222
Roon, policy of, 132, 229
Roosevelt, Miss Alice, 191
Roosevelt, President, 190-3
Rossbach, 257
Rouvier, M., 210
Rudolf of Hapsburg, 74
Russia, visit to, in 1888, 32-4; Bismarck's policy towards, 53-9, 68; the Reassurance Treaty, 58-9, 87, 95; subsequent visits to, 85, 90-1; and the appointment of Count Waldersee, 164;

INDEX

peace manifesto, 1898, 187; policy of William II towards, 203-6; attitude towards Austria, 1908-9, 231; effect of the *Entente*, 252

Russo-Japanese War, 204-6

Saalburg, the museum at, 166-8
Salisbury, Marquis of, and William II, 93; peace policy of, 187
Samoa Islands, 146-7
San Remo, 23
Sans Souci, 29
Savoy, the, 37
Saxony, 44
Scharnhorst, 229
Scheffler, Karl, 171
Schiller, estimate of William II, 10; "Wilhelm Tell" *quoted*, 55; "Cassandra" *quoted*, 159; Schiller's Day, 1905, 254
Schweninger, Prof., 62
Schwerin, 44
Sedan, 12
Serajevo, 223, 242
Serbia, the note of March 31, 1909, 231
Seymour, Admiral, 173
Shantung, murder of missionaries, 140-1
Shimoniseki, Peace of, 114-15
Siegesallee, the, 170-2
Simon, Jules, at the Labour Congress, 71-3; the conversation with William II, 71, 241 *n*.
Social Democrats, Stoecker and the, 48; William II on the, 60, 76-7, 108, 123, 149-51, 247; attitude towards the war, 238-9
Somaliland, 88
Sophia, Queen, 44
South African War, effect of German foreign policy, 147-8, 203; the concentration camps, 182; German hostility, 216

Spahn, Herr, 213
Spain, the Philippine War, 189; interests in Morocco, 209; William II and, 257
Standard, the, criticism of William II, 114-15
Stanley, H. M., on the Heligoland Agreement, 88
State Island, 190
Stead, William, 243
Stengel, Prof., 187-8
Sternburg, Speck von, 202
Stettin, 129
Stockholm, 34
Stoecker, Rev., 18, 31, 196; and Bismarck, 47-8
Stössel, General, 206
Strassburg, 127, 254
Stuttgart, 35
Sudan, the, 147
Switzerland, Germany and, 50-1

Taaffe, Count, 36, 40
Tangier, visit of William II, 208-9
Tangier affair, the, 252
Tientsin, 114
Times, The, criticism of William II, 40; on the Kruger telegram, 116; on the "Greater Germany" speech, 120
Tirpitz, Admiral von, 123-4, 140-1, 192-3
Tolstoi, 243
Trafalgar, 111
Transvaal, Jameson's raid, 115-19
Treitschke, *cited*, 55
Triple Alliance, Bismarck and the, 53; break up begun in 1901, 189
Triple Entente, offence at action of Austria, 231
Tripoli War, 1911, 189
Tsu-Hsi, Empress, 157-8
Tuileries, the, 1
Turkey, Macedonian question, 204

INDEX

Umberto ironclad, launch of the, 63
United States, overtures of William II, 189-99; German relations with, 203
Unter den Linden, 3, 12

Vatican, the, 36
Venezuela, 202-3
Vereshchagin, 205
Vernois, Herr Verdy du, 46
Versailles, the Gallery of Mirrors, 50
Vesuvius, 37
Viborg Regiment, William II and the, 205-6
Victoria, Queen, honoured by the Kaiser, 43; at Darmstadt, 84; William II and, 114-15, 147, 217; death, 118
Vienna, visits to, 35-6, 232
Virchow, 18
Voight, Wilhelm, episode of, 213-14
Vollmar, Herr von, 203
Vorwärts, the, publication of the Stoecker letter, 48-9

Waldersee, Count, 18; and Bismarck, 46-8; influence on William II, 79; mission to China, 1900, 162-4
Wartburg, 84
Washington, birthday celebrations, 190-1
Waterloo, references to, by William II, 43, 72, 201, 229
Waterloo Column, Hanover, 147
Weiland, outrage on William II, 174-7
Weimar, Duke of, 65-6
Weissenburg, 12

Weltpolitik, German, rise of, 86, 108, 120, 128, 186, 197-8
Wernigerode, 84
West, Mr. Putnam, "Indiscreet Letters from Peking," 157
Westphalia, 44
Wiesbaden, 84; speech at, 188
Wildenbruch, Ernst von, 136
Wilhelmshaven, 35, 128; speech at, 258
Wilhelmstrasse, the, 63, 219, 226
"Willehalm" play, 136-8
William I, regency, 1; and his grandson, 11-12, 14, 32; and the Franco-German War, 12; characteristics, 17-18, 77, 83; death, 23; selection of Caprivi, 61; memorial at Wernigerode, 84; celebration of the centenary of his birth, 135-8; William II on, 234-5
Windhorst, Herr, 63
Windsor Castle, 217
Wittelsbach, 128
Witu protectorate, 88
Wohlgemüth, case of, 50
Wolff's Agency, report of the Imperial Interview, 218
Wollmar, Herr, 213
Woman, William II on her duties, 247
Wörth, 12

"Yellow Book," the French, 1913, 236

Zanzibar protectorate, 88
Zeppelin, Count, 223
Zola, William II on, 71-2
Zorn, Prof., 188
Zukunft, the, 169; Harden's article *quoted*, 239